William Shakespeare's

Much Ado About Nothing

In Plain and Simple English

A SwipeSpeare ™ Book

www.SwipeSpeare.com

Table of Contents

About This Series

The "Classic Retold" series started as a way of telling classics for the modern reader—being careful to preserve the themes and integrity of the original. Whether you want to understand Shakespeare a little more or are trying to get a better grasps of the Greek classics, there is a book waiting for you!

The series is expanding every month. Visit BookCaps.com to see all the books in the series, and while you are there join the Facebook page, so you are first to know when a new book comes out.

Characters

DON PEDRO, Prince of Arragon.

DON JOHN, his bastard Brother.

CLAUDIO, a young Lord of Florence.

BENEDICK, a young Lord of Padua.

LEONATO, Governor of Messina.

ANTONIO, his Brother.

BALTHAZAR, Servant to Don Pedro.

BORACHIO, follower of Don John.

CONRADE, follower of Don John.

DOGBERRY, a Constable.

VERGES, a Headborough.

FRIAR FRANCIS.

A Sexton.

A Boy.

HERO, Daughter to Leonato

BEATRICE, Niece to Leonato

MARGARET, Waiting-gentlewoman attending on Hero.

URSULA, Waiting-gentlewoman attending on Hero.

Messengers, Watch, Attendants, &c.

SCENE. Messina.

Play

Act I

Scene I

Before LEONATO'S House.

[Enter LEONATO, HERO, BEATRICE and others, with a Messenger.]

LEONATO
I learn in this letter that Don Pedro of Arragon comes this night to Messina.

This letter says that Don Pedro of Arragon is coming to Messina tonight.

MESSENGER
He is very near by this:
he was not three leagues off when I left him.

*He is very near this place:
he was less than three leagues away when I left him.*

LEONATO
How many gentlemen have you lost in this action?

How many noblemen have you lost in combat?

MESSENGER
But few of any sort, and none of name.

Only a few of any kind, and no famous ones.

LEONATO
A victory is twice itself when the achiever brings home full numbers. I find here that Don Pedro hath bestowed much honour on a young Florentine called Claudio.

A victory is twice as good when the person who achieves victory brings home all the soldiers. I read here that Don Pedro has given much honor to a young Florentine called Claudio.

MESSENGER
Much deserved on his part, and equally remembered by Don Pedro. He hath borne himself beyond the promise of his age, doing in the figure of a lamb the feats of a lion: he hath indeed better bettered expectation than you must expect of me to tell you how.

He deserves the honor, and this is well-remembered by Don Pedro. He has carried himself beyond what one would expect from someone his age, and though he seems like a lamb he has the accomplishments of a lion: he has indeed done a better job exceeding expectations than you can expect me to tell you how.

LEONATO
He hath an uncle here in Messina will be very much glad of it.

He has an uncle here in Messina that will be very much glad of it.

MESSENGER
I have already delivered him letters, and there appears much joy in him; even so much that joy could not show itself modest enough without a badge of bitterness.

I have already delivered him letters, and he seems very pleased, so much so that he could not express it without what is usually a sign of sadness.

LEONATO
Did he break out into tears?

Did he burst into tears?

MESSENGER
In great measure.

A great deal.

LEONATO
A kind overflow of kindness. There are no faces truer than those that are so washed; how much better is it to weep at joy than to joy at weeping!

A kind overflowing of kindness. There are no faces more honest than ones washed with tears; it is much better to cry from joy than enjoy others' crying!

BEATRICE
I pray you, is Signior Mountanto returned from the wars or no?

Please tell me, is Sir Mountanto returned from the wars or no?

MESSENGER
I know none of that name, lady:
there was none such in the army of any sort.

I do not know anyone with that name, lady: there was no man of any kind named that in the army.

LEONATO
What is he that you ask for, niece?

Who is he you are asking after, my niece?

HERO
My cousin means Signior Benedick of Padua.

My cousin means Sir Benedick of Padua.

MESSENGER
O! he is returned, and as pleasant as ever he was.

Oh! He has returned, and he is as pleasant as he ever was.

BEATRICE
He set up his bills here in Messina and challenged Cupid at the flight; and my uncle's fool, reading the challenge, subscribed for Cupid, and challenged him at the bird-bolt. I pray you, how many hath he killed and eaten in these wars? But how many hath he killed? for, indeed, I promised to eat all of his killing.

He stayed here for a while in Messina and challenged Cupid at the escape; and my uncle's jester, reading the challenge, took Cupid's side, and challenged him in bird hunting. Please tell me, how many has he killed and eaten in these wars? But how many has he killed? for, indeed, I promised to eat all the birds he killed.

LEONATO
Faith, niece, you tax Signior Benedick too much; but he'll be meet with you, I doubt it not.

My goodness, niece, you ask too much of Sir Benedick; but he'll be fair with you, I have no doubt.

MESSENGER
He hath done good service, lady, in these wars.

He has served us well, lady, in these wars.

BEATRICE
You had musty victual, and he hath holp to eat it;

You had a lot of food, and he hopes to eat it;

eat it; he is a very valiant trencher-man; he hath an excellent stomach.

MESSENGER
And a good soldier too, lady.

BEATRICE
And a good soldier to a lady; but what is he to a lord?

MESSENGER
A lord to a lord, a man to a man; stuffed with all honourable virtues.

BEATRICE
It is so indeed; he is no less than a stuffed man; but for the stuffing,--well, we are all mortal.

LEONATO
You must not, sir, mistake my niece. There is a kind of merry war betwixt Signior Benedick and her; they never meet but there's a skirmish of wit between them.

BEATRICE
Alas! he gets nothing by that. In our last conflict four of his five wits went halting off, and now is the whole man governed with one! so that if he have wit enough to keep himself warm, let him bear it for a difference between himself and his horse; for it is all the wealth that he hath left to be known a reasonable creature. Who is his companion now? He hath every month a new sworn brother.

MESSENGER
Is't possible?

BEATRICE
Very easily possible: he wears his faith but as the fashion of his hat; it ever changes with the next block.

MESSENGER

I see, lady, the gentleman is not in your books.

---

he is a big eater; he has an excellent stomach.

And he is a good soldier too, lady.

He may be a good soldier to a lady; but what is he to a lord?

He is a lord to a lord, a man to a man; stuffed with all honorable virtues.

That is true; he is no less than a stuffed man; but as for the stuffing - well, we are all human.

Sir, you must not misunderstand my niece. There is a kind of friendly rivalry between Sir Benedick and her; they never meet without a battle of cleverness between them.

Unfortunately, he gets nothing out of it. In our last conflict four of his five senses left him, and now the whole man only has one! So if he has enough intelligence left to keep himself warm, let him keep it in order to make a difference between himself and his horse; for it is all the wealth he has left to be known as a creature of reason. Who is his companion now? Every month he has a new best friend.

Is it possible?

Very easily possible: he wears his loyalty like he wears his hat a certain way; it constantly changes with the next period of time.

I see, lady, the gentleman is not in your good

	books.

BEATRICE
No;an he were, I would burn my study. But, I pray you, who is his companion? Is there no young squarer now that will make a voyage with him to the devil?

No; if he were, I would burn my library. But, please tell me, who is is companion? Is there no young squire now that will travel with him to the devil?

MESSENGER
He is most in the company of the right noble Claudio.

He is most often in the company of the noble Claudio.

BEATRICE
O Lord, he will hang upon him like a disease: he is sooner caught than the pestilence, and the taker runs presently mad. God help the noble Claudio! If he have caught the Benedick, it will cost him a thousand pound ere a' be cured.

Oh Lord, he will hang around him like a disease: he is more easily caught than an infection, and the infected soon becomes insane. God help the noble Claudio! If he has caught the Benedick, it will cost him a thousand pounds [of money] before he is cured.

MESSENGER
I will hold friends with you, lady.

I will agree to disagree with you, lady.

BEATRICE
Do, good friend.

Do, my good friend.

LEONATO
You will never run mad, niece.

You will never be that fond of Benedick, niece.

BEATRICE
No, not till a hot January.

No, not until there is a hot January.

MESSENGER
Don Pedro is approached.

Don Pedro is here.

[Enter DON PEDRO, DON JOHN, CLAUDIO, BENEDICK, BALTHAZAR, and Others.]

DON PEDRO
Good Signior Leonato, you are come to meet your trouble: the fashion of the world is to avoid cost, and you encounter it.

Good Sir Leonato, you have come to meet your trouble: the world prefers to avoid cost, and you encounter it.

LEONATO
Never came trouble to my house in the likeness of your Grace,
for trouble being gone, comfort should remain;
but when you depart from me, sorrow abides

*Trouble never came to my house looking like your Grace,
for once trouble goes, comfort should remain;
but when you leave me, sorrow stays and*

and happiness takes his leave.

happiness goes away.

DON PEDRO
You embrace your charge too willingly.
I think this is your daughter.

You are too kind. I think this is your daughter.

LEONATO
Her mother hath many times told me so.

Her mother has told me so many times.

BENEDICK
Were you in doubt, sir, that you asked her?

Did you ask her because you were in doubt, sir?

LEONATO
Signior Benedick, no; for then were you a child.

No, Sir Benedick; for at the time you were a child.

DON PEDRO
You have it full, Benedick: we may guess by this
what you are, being a man. Truly the lady fathers
herself. Be happy, lady, for you are like an
honourable father.

You have the whole story, Benedick: we may guess by this what you are, being a man. Truly the lady looks enough like her father for people to tell. Be happy, lady, for you resemble an honorable father.

BENEDICK
If Signior Leonato be her father, she would not
have his head on her shoulders for all Messina,
as like him as she is.

If Sir Leonato is her father, she would not have his head on her shoulders in exchange for all Messina, no matter how much she is like him.

BEATRICE
I wonder that you will still be talking, Signior
Benedick: nobody marks you.

I am amazed that you are still talking, Sir Benedick: nobody is listening to you.

BENEDICK
What! my dear Lady Disdain, are you yet living?

What! my dear Lady Disapproval, are you still alive?

BEATRICE
Is it possible Disdain should die while she hath
such meet food to feed it as Signior Benedick?
Courtesy itself must convert to disdain if you
come in her presence.

Is it possible Disapproval could die while she had such appropriate food to feed it as Sir Benedick? Politeness itself must turn to disapproval if you come in her presence.

BENEDICK
Then is courtesy a turncoat. But it is certain I am
loved of all ladies, only you excepted; and I
would I could find in my heart that I had not a
hard heart;for, truly, I love none.
BEATRICE
A dear happiness to women: they would else

Then politeness is a traitor. But it is certain that all the ladies love me, except for you; and I wish I could find it in myself to not be hard-hearted; for, truly, I love none.

That is very good for women: otherwise they

have been troubled with a pernicious suitor.
I thank God and my cold blood, I am of your
humour for that. I had rather hear my dog bark
at a crow than a man swear he loves me.

*would have been troubled by a terrible suitor.
I thank God and my cold blood, I am of your
temperament for that. I would rather hear my
dog bark at a crow than a man swear he loves
me.*

BENEDICK
God keep your ladyship still in that mind;
so some gentleman or other shallscape a
predestinate scratched face.

*May God keep your ladyship from changing
your mind; so some gentleman or other shall
escape a scratched face that would otherwise
be his destiny.*

BEATRICE
Scratching could not make it worse, an 'twere
such a face as yours were.

*Scratching could not make it worse, if it was a
face like yours.*

BENEDICK
Well, you are a rare parrot-teacher.

*Well, you are an unusually good parrot-
teacher.*

BEATRICE
A bird of my tongue is better than a beast of yours.

*A bird with my tongue would be better than a
beast with yours.*

BENEDICK
I would my horse had the speed of your tongue,
and so good a continuer. But keep your way,
i' God's name; I have done.

*I wish my horse was as fast as your tongue,
and had the same amound of endurance. But
have it your way, in God's name; I am done.*

BEATRICE
You always end with a jade's trick:
I know you of old.

*You always end with a cheap trick:
I've known you for a long time.*

DON PEDRO
That is the sum of all, Leonato: Signior Claudio,
and Signior Benedick, my dear friend Leonato
hath invited you all. I tell him we shall stay
here at the least a month, and he heartly prays
some occasion may detain us longer: I dare
swear he is no hypocrite, but prays from his heart.

*To sum it up, Leonato: Sir Claudio, and Sir
Benedick, my dear friend Leonato has invited
you all. I tell him we shall stay at least a
month, and he strongly hopes that for
some reason we will stay longer. I believe
he is no hypocrite, but genuinely means it.*

LEONATO
If you swear, my lord, you shall not be forsworn.
[To DON JOHN]
Let me bid you welcome, my lord: being
reconciled to the prince your brother,
I owe you all duty.
DON JOHN
I thank you: I am not of many words,
but I thank you.

*If you promise, my lord, you will not be
forgotten. [To DON JOHN]
Let me welcome you, my lord; as I accept
being a subject of your brother the prince, I
owe you my loyalty.*

*I thank you: I am not very talkative,
but I thank you.*

LEONATO
Please it your Grace lead on?

DON PEDRO
Your hand, Leonato; we will go together.

[Exeunt all but BENEDICK and CLAUDIO.]

[Exit all but BENEDICK and CLAUDIO.]

CLAUDIO
Benedick, didst thou note the daughter of
Signior Leonato?

BENEDICK
I noted her not; but I looked on her.

CLAUDIO
Is she not a modest young lady?

BENEDICK
Do you question me, as an honest man should do,
for my simple true judgment; or would you have
me speak after my custom, as being a professed
tyrant to their sex?

CLAUDIO
No; I pray thee speak in sober judgment.

BENEDICK
Why, i' faith, methinks she's too low for a high
praise, too brown for a fair praise, and too little
for a great praise; only this commendation I can
afford her, that were she other than she is, she
were unhandsome, and being no other but as
she is, I do not like her.

CLAUDIO
Thou thinkest I am in sport: I pray thee tell me
truly how thou likest her.

BENEDICK
Would you buy her, that you enquire after her?

CLAUDIO

Would your Grace please lead us onward?

*Give me your hand, Leonato; we will go
together.*

*Benedick, did you notice the daughter of Sir
Leonato?*

*I did not really notice her; but I did look at
her.*

Isn't she a proper, humble young lady?

*Are you asking me, as an honest man should
do, for my simple true judgment; or would
you like me to speak like I usually do, as a
claimed hater of the whole gender of women?*

*No; please speak in calm and rational
judgment.*

*Why, by my faith, I think she is too short to be
praised as tall, too dark to be praised as
fair-skinned, and too little to be praised as
large; I can only offer this praise, that if she
were other than she is, she would not be
attractive, and being nothing more than she is,
I do not like her.*

*You think I am joking: please tell me
truly if you like her.*

*Do you want to buy her, asking about her like
this?*

Can the world buy such a jewel?

Can the world buy a jewel like her?

BENEDICK
Yea, and a case to put it into. But speak you this with a sad brow, or do you play the flouting Jack, to tell us Cupid is a good hare-finder, and Vulcan a rare carpenter? Come, in what key shall a man take you, to go in the song?

Yes, and a case to put it into. But are you saying this with a sad face, or are you acting as a ladies' man, to tell us Cupid is good at finding rabbits, and Vulcan [the Roman god of ironwork and smiths] an unusually good carpenter? Come, in what [musical] key shall a man take you, to burst into song?

CLAUDIO
In mine eye she is the sweetest lady that ever I looked on.

In my eyes she is the sweetest lady I have ever gazed upon.

BENEDICK
I can see yet without spectacles and I see no such matter: there's her cousin an she were not possessed with a fury, exceeds her as much in beauty as the first of May doth the last of December. But I hope you have no intent to turn husband, have you?

I can still see without glasses and I see no such thing: there's her cousin if she were not constantly angry, is more beautiful than her as much as the first of May is more beautiful than the last of December. But I hope you don't mean to become a husband, do you?

CLAUDIO
I would scarce trust myself, though I had sworn to the contrary, if Hero would be my wife.

I would hardly trust myself, even if I had sworn against it, if Hero would be my wife.

BENEDICK
Is't come to this, i' faith? Hath not the world one man but he will wear his cap with suspicion? Shall I never see a bachelor of threescore again? Go to, i' faith; an thou wilt needs thrust thy neck into a yoke, wear the print of it and sigh away Sundays. Look! Don Pedro is returned to seek you.

Is it to come to this, by my faith? Does the world only have one man who will stay single? Shall I never see a thirty-year-old bachelor again? Enough, by my faith, and you will have to stick your neck into an ox's harness, wear the mark of it and be imprisoned and regretful for the rest of your life. Look! Don Pedro is back to look for you.

[Re-enter DON PEDRO.]

DON PEDRO
What secret hath held you here, that you followed not to Leonato's?

What secret has kept you here, that you did not follow to Leonato's?

BENEDICK
I would your Grace would constrain me to tell.

I would prefer your Grace to demand me to tell.

DON PEDRO

I charge thee on thy allegiance.

I charge you by your allegiance.

BENEDICK
You hear, Count Claudio: I can be secret as a dumb man; I would have you think so; but on my allegiance mark you this, on my allegiance: he is in love. With who? now that is your Grace's part. Mark how short his answer is: with Hero, Leonato's short daughter.

You hear, Count Claudio: I can be as secret as a man who cannot speak; I would have you think so; but on my allegiance know this, on my allegiance: he is in love. With who? Now that is your Grace's part. Notice how short his answer is: with Hero, Leonato's short daughter.

CLAUDIO
If this were so, so were it uttered.

If this was true, that is how it would be said.

BENEDICK
Like the old tale, my lord: 'it is not so, nor 'twas not so; but indeed, God forbid it should be so.'

Like in the old story, my lord: 'it is not true, it never was true; but indeed, God forbid that it should be true.'

CLAUDIO
If my passion change not shortly.
God forbid it should be otherwise.

If my feelings do not soon change.
God forbid it should be otherwise.

DON PEDRO
Amen, if you love her; for the lady is very well worthy.

Amen, if you love her; for she is a very worthwhile lady.

CLAUDIO
You speak this to fetch me in, my lord.

You are teasing me, my lord.

DON PEDRO
By my troth, I speak my thought.

I swear by the truth, I am speaking my thoughts.

CLAUDIO
And in faith, my lord, I spoke mine.

And by my faith, my lord, I spoke mine.

BENEDICK
And by my two faiths and troths, my lord, I spoke mine.

And by my two faiths and two truths, my lord, I spoke mine.

CLAUDIO
That I love her, I feel.

I feel that I love her.

DON PEDRO
That she is worthy, I know.

I know that she is worthy.

BENEDICK
That I neither feel how she should be loved nor

Fire could not melt the opinion out of me;

know how she should be worthy, is the opinion
that fire cannot melt out of me: I will die in it
at the stake.

I neither feel how she could be loved or know how she could be worthy: I will die of being burned at the stake.

DON PEDRO
Thou wast ever an obstinate heretic in the despite
of beauty.

You always were a stubborn heretic despite all beauty.

CLAUDIO
And never could maintain his part but in the
force of his will.

And never could hold onto his position except by force of will.

BENEDICK
That a woman conceived me, I thank her; that
she brought me up, I likewise give her most
humble thanks; but that I will have a recheat
winded in my forehead, or hang my bugle in an
invisible baldrick, all women shall pardon me.
Because I will not do them the wrong to mistrust
any, I will do myself the right to trust none;
and the fine is,--for the which I may go the finer,
--I will live a bachelor.

That a woman gave birth to me, I thank her; that she raised me, I similarly give my most humble thanks; but that I would stop being a free man, all women should forgive me if I said no. Because I will not do them the wrong to distrust any, I will do myself the right to trust none; and what it all boils down to is that I will live a bachelor.

DON PEDRO
I shall see thee, ere I die, look pale with love.

I will see you, before I die, look pale with love.

BENEDICK
With anger, with sickness, or with hunger,
my lord; not with love: prove that ever I lose
more blood with love than I will get again with
drinking, pick out mine eyes with a ballad-maker's
pen and hang me up at the door of a brothel-house
for the sign of blind Cupid.

With anger, with sickness, or with hunger, my lord; not with love: and if I ever lose more blood with love than I will get again with drinking, pick out my eyes with a poet's pen and hang me up at the door of a whorehouse to represent blind Cupid.

DON PEDRO
Well, if ever thou dost fall from this faith,
thou wilt prove a notable argument.

Well, if you ever do change your mind, you will be a notable argument.

BENEDICK.
If I do, hang me in a bottle like a cat and shoot
at me;
and he that hits me, let him be clapped on the
shoulder and called Adam.

*If I do, hang me in a bottle like a cat and shoot at me;
and the man that hits me should be cheered and congratulated.*

DON PEDRO
Well, as time shall try: 'In time the savage bull

Well, as time will tell: "In time the savage

doth bear the yoke.'

bull shall carry the yoke."

BENEDICK
The savage bull may; but if ever the sensible Benedick bear it, pluck off the bull's horns and set them in my forehead; and let me be vilely painted, and in such great letters as they write, 'Here is good horse to hire,' let them signify under my sign 'Here you may see Benedick the married man.'

The savage bull may; but if the sensible Benedick ever carries it, pluck off the bull's horns and attach them to my forehead; and let me be garishly painted, and in such huge letters as they write "Here is a good horse to hire," let them write under my sign "Here you may see Benedick the married man."

CLAUDIO
If this should ever happen, thou wouldst be horn-mad.

If this ever happened, you would be crazy with passion.

DON PEDRO
Nay, if Cupid have not spent all his quiver in Venice, thou wilt quake for this shortly.

No, if Cupid has not used up all his arrows in Venice, you will quake for this shortly.

BENEDICK
I look for an earthquake too then.

That is as likely as an earthquake.

DON PEDRO
Well, you will temporize with the hours. In the meantime, good Signior Benedick, repair to Leonato's: commend me to him and tell him I will not fail him at supper; for indeed he hath made great preparation.

Well, give it time. Meanwhile, good Sir Benedick, go to Leonato's: thank him for me and tell him I will certainly be at supper; for indeed he has made much preparation.

BENEDICK
I have almost matter enough in me for such an embassage; and so I commit you--

I almost have enough in me to deliver such a message; and so I commit you –

CLAUDIO
To the tuition of God: from my house, if I had it,--

[Pretending that Benedick is writing a letter.] To the tuition of God: from my house, if I had it, -

DON PEDRO
The sixth of July: your loving friend, Benedick.

[Joining in the game.] The sixty of July: your loving friend, Benedick.

BENEDICK
Nay, mock not, mock not. The body of your discourse is sometime guarded with fragments, and the guards are but slightly basted on neither: ere you flout old ends any further, examine your conscience: and so I leave you.

No, do not make fun of me, really. The main portion of your conversations is sometimes guarded with fragments, and the guards are only slightly meaningless: before you tease about old endings any further, examine your conscience: and so I leave you.

[Exit.]

CLAUDIO
My liege, your highness now may do me good.

Sir, your highness may now do me good.

DON PEDRO
My love is thine to teach: teach it but how,

My affection for you can do anything: just tell me how,

And thou shalt see how apt it is to learn hard lesson that may do thee good.

And you shall see how useful it is to learn a hard lesson that may do you good.

CLAUDIO
Hath Leonato any son, my lord?

Does Leonato have any son, my lord?

DON PEDRO
No child but Hero; she's his only heir.
Dost thou affect her, Claudio?

*No child but Hero; she's his only heir.
Are you fond of her, Claudio?*

CLAUDIO
O! my lord,
When you went onward on this ended action,

*Oh, my lord,
When you began this recently completed action,*

I looked upon her with a soldier's eye,
That lik'd, but had a rougher task in hand
Than to drive liking to the name of love;
But now I am return'd, and that war-thoughts

*I looked at her the way a soldier would,
That liked, but had a rougher job to do
Than to pursue my liking and turn it to love;
But now I have returned, and now that war-thoughts*

Have left their places vacant, in their rooms

Have left their places empty, and in their old rooms

Come thronging soft and delicate desires,
All prompting me how fair young Hero is,
Saying, I lik'd her ere I went to wars.

*Soft and delicate desires come crowding,
All telling me how beautiful young Hero is,
Saying I liked her before I went to wars.*

DON PEDRO
Thou wilt be like a lover presently,
And tire the hearer with a book of words.

*You will soon be like a lover,
And exhaust your listeners with a book's worth of words.*

If thou dost love fair Hero, cherish it,
And I will break with her, and with her father,
And thou shalt have her.
Was't not to this end
That thou began'st to twist so fine a story?

*If you do love beautiful Hero, cherish it,
And I will tell her, and her father,
And you shall have her.
Wasn't this the reason
That you began to tell me such a pretty story?*

CLAUDIO
How sweetly you do minister to love,

How sweetly you treat love,

That know love's grief by his complexion!

But lest my liking might too sudden seem,
I would have salv'd it with a longer treatise.

DON PEDRO
What need the bridge much broader than the flood?

The fairest grant is the necessity.
Look, what will serve is fit: 'tis once, thou lov'st,

And I will fit thee with the remedy.
I know we shall have revelling to-night:
I will assume thy part in some disguise,
And tell fair Hero I am Claudio;
And in her bosom I'll unclasp my heart,
And take her hearing prisoner with the force
And strong encounter of my amorous tale:
Then, after to her father will I break;
And the conclusion is, she shall be thine.
In practice let us put it presently.

[Exeunt.]

You that know love's grief by his facial expression!
But in case my liking might seem too sudden,
I would have made a longer speech to salvage it.

Why should the bridge be much wider than the river?
The best reason for anything is necessity.
Look, we will go with whatever works: it is once, that you love,
And I will provide you with a solution.
I know we shall have dancing tonight:
I will pretend to be you in some disguise,
And tell beautiful Hero that I am Claudio;
And bring our hearts together,
And convince her with the force
And strength of my romantic tale:
Then, I will tell her father afterwards;
And the conclusion is, she shall be yours.
Let us quickly put this into practice.

Scene II

A room in LEONATO'S house

[Enter LEONATO and ANTONIO, meeting.]

LEONATO
How now, brother! Where is my cousin
your son? Hath he provided this music?

*Good to see you, brother! Where is my cousin,
your son? Has he provided this music?*

ANTONIO
He is very busy about it. But, brother, I can tell
you strange news that you yet dreamt not of.

*He is very busy with it. But, brother, I can tell
you strange news that you never dreamed of.*

LEONATO
Are they good?

Is it good news?

ANTONIO
As the event stamps them: but they have a good
cover; they show well outward. The prince and
Count Claudio, walking in a thick-pleached alley
in my orchard, were thus much overheard by a
man of mine: the prince discovered to Claudio
that he loved my niece your daughter and meant
to acknowledge it this night in a dance; and if
he found her accordant, he meant to take the
present time by the top and instantly break with
you of it.

*It seems to be that way: at least they
outwardly appear well. The prince and
Count Claudio, walking in a shaded alley
in my orchard, were overheard talking by
a man of mine: the prince told Claudio that
he loved my niece, your daughter, and meant
to announce it tonight in a dance; and if
he found her willing, he meant to seize the
moment and instantly let you know.*

LEONATO
Hath the fellow any wit that told you this?

Is the man who told you this a sensible one?

ANTONIO
A good sharp fellow: I will send for him;
and question him yourself.

*A good sharp fellow: I will ask him to come;
and you can question him yourself.*

LEONATO
No, no; we will hold it as a dream till it appear
itself: but I will acquaint my daughter withal,
that she may be the better prepared for an
answer, if peradventure this be true. Go you,
and tell her of it.
[Several persons cross the stage.]
Cousins, you know what you have to do.
O! I cry you mercy, friend; go you with me,

*No, no; we will treat it like a dream until it
appears as reality: but I will tell my daughter
of this, so that she will be prepared for an
answer, if eventually this turns out to be true.
You go and tell her about it.*

*Relatives, you know what you have to do.
Oh! I plead with you, friend; come with me,*

and I will use your skill. Good cousin,
have a care this busy time.
[Exeunt]

and I will use your skill. Good cousin,
take care during this busy time.

Scene III

Another room in LEONATO'S house.

[Enter DON JOHN and CONRADE.]

CONRADE
What the good-year, my lord! why are you thus
out of measure sad?

*What on earth, my lord! Why are you so
unreasonably sad?*

DON JOHN
There is no measure in the occasion that breeds;
therefore the sadness is without limit.

*There is nothing in this particular occasion
that causes it; therefore the sadness is without
limit.*

CONRADE
You should hear reason.

You should be reasonable.

DON JOHN
And when I have heard it,
what blessings brings it?

*And if I choose to hear reason,
what good does it do me?*

CONRADE
If not a present remedy,
at least a patient sufferance.

*If not an immediate solution,
it might at least help you bear it patiently.*

DON JOHN
I wonder that thou, being, -as thou say'st
thou art,--born under Saturn, goest about to
apply a moral medicine to a mortifying
mischief. I cannot hide what I am: I must be sad
when I have cause, and smile at no man's jests;
eat when I have stomach, and wait for no man's
leisure; sleep when I am drowsy, and tend on
no man's business; laugh when I am merry,
and claw no man in his humour.

*I am surprised by you being so optimistic,
trying to impose morality on me. I cannot
hide what I am [an illegitimate son]:
I must be sad when I have a reason to, and
smile at no man's jokes; eat when I am
hungry, and wait for no man's leisure;
sleep when I am drowsy, and follow no man's
business; laugh when I am cheerful, and not
go by the moods of someone else.*

CONRADE
Yea; but you must not make the full show of this
till you may do it without controlment. You have
of late stood out against your brother, and he
hath ta'en you newly into his grace; where it is
impossible you should take true root but by the
fair weather that you make yourself:

*Yes, but you must not be too obvious about it
until you may do it freely. You have lately
stood out against your brother, and he has
recently brought you into his favor once more;
where it is impossible for you to succeed
except by the good circumstances you make*

it is needful that you frame the season for your own harvest.

yourself: it is necessary that you bright about the season for your own harvest.

DON JOHN
I had rather be a canker in a hedge than a rose in his grace; and it better fits my blood to be disdained of all than to fashion a carriage to rob love from any: in this, though I cannot be said to be a flattering honest man, it must not be denied but I am a plain-dealing villain. I am trusted with a muzzle and enfranchised with a clog; therefore I have decreed not to sing in my cage. If I had my mouth, I would bite; if I had my liberty, I would do my liking: in the meantime, let me be that I am, and seek not to alter me.

I would rather be a thorn in a hedge than a rose in his favor; and it better fits my blood to be hated by all than to find a way to rob love from any: in this, though I cannot be said to be a flattering honest man, it must not be denied that I am a plain and simple villain. I am kept silent and condemned to poverty therefore I have decided not to sing in my cage. If I had my mouth, I would bite; if I had my liberty, I would do as I liked: in the meantime, let me be what I am, and do not try to change me.

CONRADE
Can you make no use of your discontent?

Can't you do something useful with your unhappiness?

DON JOHN
I make all use of it, for I use it only.
Who comes here?
[Enter Borachio.]
What news, Borachio?

It is the only thing I use it all.
Who comes here?

What news [do you have], Borachio?

BORACHIO
I came yonder from a great supper: the prince your brother is royally entertained by Leonato; and I can give you intelligence of an intended marriage.

I came here from a lavish dinner: the prince, your brother, is royally entertained by Leonato; and I can give you information about an intended marriage.

DON JOHN
Will it serve for any model to build mischief on? What is he for a fool that betroths himself to unquietness?

Is it something that I can use to cause mischief? Who is he, the fool that is condemning himself to the chaos of having a wife?

BORACHIO
Marry, it is your brother's right hand.

Why, it is your brother's right-hand man.

DON JOHN
Who? the most exquisite Claudio?

Who? The 'wonderful' Claudio?

BORACHIO
Even he.

Yes, him.

DON JOHN

A proper squire! And who, and who?
which way looks he?

A proper gentleman! And who is he interested in?

BORACHIO
Marry, on Hero, the daughter and heir of Leonato.

Why, Hero, the daughter and heir of Leonato.

DON JOHN
A very forward March-chick!
How came you to this?

*A very daring young person!
How did you learn about this?*

BORACHIO
Being entertained for a perfumer, as I was
smoking a musty room, comes me the prince
and Claudio, hand in hand, in sad conference:
I whipt me behind the arras, and there heard it
agreed upon that the prince should woo Hero
for himself, and having obtained her, give her
to Count Claudio.

*As I was smoking, the prince and Claudio
came in my direction, hand in hand, for a
serious meeting: I hid behind the stairs, and
there I heard it agreed that the prince would
woo Hero for himself, and having got her,
give her to Count Claudio.*

DON JOHN
Come, come; let us thither: this may prove food
to my displeasure. That young start-up hath all the
glory of my overthrow: if I can cross him any way,
I bless myself every way. You are both sure, and
will assist me?

*Let us go: this may give my displeasure
something to feed upon. That young start-up
will bring glory to my overthrowing him: if I
can wrong him in any way, I bless myself in
every way. You are both sure, and will assist
me?*

CONRADE
To the death, my lord.

Even to the death, my lord.

DON JOHN
Let us to the great supper: their cheer is the
greater that I am subdued. Would the cook were
of my mind! Shall we go to prove what's to be
done?

*Let us go eat at the great supper: their
cheerfulness is even better when I am
subdued. If only the cook agreed with me!
Shall we go to find out what is to be done?*

BORACHIO
We'll wait upon your lordship.

We will serve your lordship.

[Exeunt.]

Act II

Scene I

A hall in LEONATO'S house.

[Enter LEONATO, ANTONIO, HERO, BEATRICE, and Others.]

LEONATO
Was not Count John here at supper?

Wasn't Count John here at supper?

ANTONIO
I saw him not.

I did not see him.

BEATRICE
How tartly that gentleman looks! I never can
see him but I am heart-burned an hour after.

How sour that gentleman looks!
Whenever I see him I have heartburn even an
hour after.

HERO
He is of a very melancholy disposition.

He has a very melancholy personality.

BEATRICE
He were an excellent man that were made just in
the mid-way between him and Benedick:
the one is too like an image, and says nothing;
and the other too like my lady's eldest son,
evermore tattling.

He would be an excellent man, a man that was
made exactly midway between him and
Benedick: one is too much like a statue, and
says nothing; and the other too much like my
lady's eldest son, constantly talking.

LEONATO
Then half Signior Benedick's tongue in Count
John's mouth, and half Count John's melancholy
in Signior Benedick's face,--

Then half Sir Benedick's tongue in Count
John's mouth, and half Count John's
melancholy in Sir Benedick's face, -

BEATRICE
With a good leg and a good foot, uncle, and
money enough in his purse, such a man would
win any woman in the world ifa' could get her
good will.

With some dancing skills, uncle, and enough
money, such a man would win any woman in
the world if only he could get her goodwill.

LEONATO
By my troth, niece, thou wilt never get thee a
husband, if thou be so shrewd of thy tongue.

My goodness, niece, you will never get
yourself a husband, if you are so sharp in
your talking.

ANTONIO
In faith, she's too curst.
BEATRICE

Indeed, she's too cursed.

Too curst is more than curst: I shall lessen
God's sending that way; for it is said, 'God
sends a curst cow short horns;' but to a cow
too curst he sends none.

LEONATO
So, by being too curst,
God will send you no horns?

BEATRICE
Just, if he send me no husband; for the which
blessing I am at him upon my knees every
morning and evening. Lord! I could not endure
a husband with a beard on his face: I had
rather lie in the woollen.

LEONATO
You may light on a husband that hath no beard.

BEATRICE
What should I do with him? dress him in my
apparel and make him my waiting-gentlewoman?
He that hath a beard is more than a youth, and
he that hath no beard is less than a man; and he
that is more than a youth is not for me; and he
that is less than a man, I am not for him:
therefore I will even take sixpence in earnest of
the bear-ward, and lead his apes into hell.

LEONATO
Well then, go you into hell?

BEATRICE
No; but to the gate; and there will the devil meet
me, like an old cuckold, with horns on his head,
and say, 'Get you to heaven, Beatrice, get you
to heaven; here's no place for you maids: 'so
deliver I up my apes, and away to Saint Peter
for the heavens; he shows me where the
bachelors sit, and there live we as merry as the
day is long.

ANTONIO
[To Hero.] Well, niece, I trust you will be ruled
by your father.
BEATRICE

---

*Too cursed is more than cursed: I shall reduce
what God sends that way; for it is said, 'God
sends a cursed cow short horns,' but to a cow
too cursed he sends none.*

*So, by being too cursed,
God will send you no horns?*

*Just that, if he send me no husband; for which
blessing I pray in thanks to him upon my
knees every morning and evening. Lord!
I could not endure a husband with a beard
on his face: I would rather be poor.*

*You may end up with a husband that has no
beard.*

*What should I do with him? Dress him in my
clothes and make him my lady-in-waiting?
He that has a beard is more than a youth, and
he that has no beard is less than a man; and
he that is more than a youth is not for me;
and he that is less than a man, I am not for
him: therefore I will accept a small sum of
money and lead his apes into hell.*

Well then, do you go into hell?

*No, but to the gate; and there will the devil
meet me, like an old man with an adulterous
wife, and say, 'Go to heaven, Beatrice, go to
heaven; this is no place for you unmarried
women." So I deliver up my apes, and away to
Saint Peter for the heavens; he shows me
where the bachelors sit, and we live there as
happily as the day is long.*

Well, niece, I trust you will obey your father.

Yes, faith; it is my cousin's duty to make curtsy, and say, 'Father, as it please you:'— but yet for all that, cousin, let him be a handsome fellow, or else make another curtsy, and say, 'Father, as it please me.'

LEONATO
Well, niece,
I hope to see you one day fitted with a husband.

BEATRICE
Not till God make men of some other metal than earth. Would it not grieve a woman to be over-mastered with a piece of valiant dust? to make an account of her life to a clod of wayward marl? No, uncle, I'll none: Adam's sons are my brethren; and truly, I hold it a sin to match in my kinred.

LEONATO
Daughter, remember what I told you: if the prince do solicit you in that kind, you know your answer.

BEATRICE
The fault will be in the music, cousin, if you be not wooed in good time: if the prince be too important, tell him there is measure in everything, and so dance out the answer. For, hear me, Hero: wooing, wedding, and repenting is as a Scotch jig, a measure, and a cinque- pace: the first suit is hot and hasty, like a Scotch jig, and full as fantastical; the wedding, mannerly-modest, as a measure, full of state and ancientry; and then comes Repentance, and with his bad legs, falls into the cinque-pace faster and faster, till he sink into his grave.

LEONATO
Cousin, you apprehend passing shrewdly.

BEATRICE
I have a good eye, uncle:
I can see a church by daylight.
LEONATO
The revellers are entering, brother:

Yes, by my faith; it is my cousin's duty to curtsy, and say, 'Father, as it pleases you.' But yet for all that, cousin, let him be a handsome fellow, or else make a different curtsy, and say, 'Father, as it pleases me.'

Well, niece,
I hope to see you one day supplied with a husband.

Not until God makes men of some other material than dirt. Wouldn't it cause sorrow sorrow to a woman to be ruled over with a piece of brave dust? To make an account of her life to a clod of wayward soil? No, uncle, I'll have none: Adam's sons are my brothers; and truly, I think it is a sin to commit incest like that.

Daughter, remember what I told you: if the prince does show interest in you in that way, you know your answer.

The fault will be in the music, cousin, if you are not courted quickly: if the prince thinks himself too important, tell him there is moderation in everything, and so dance out the answer. For, here me, Hero: wooing, wedding, and regretting is like a Scotch jig, a measure, and a five-step: the first part is hot and hasty, like a Scotch jig, and fully fantastical; the wedding, modest and mannerly as a measure, full of dignity and tradition; and then comes Regret, and with his bad legs, falls into the five-step faster and faster, until he sinks into his grave.

My relative, you have a clever view of death.

I have good vision, uncle:
I can see a church by daylight.

The partiers are entering, brother:

make good room.

give them room.

[Enter, DON PEDRO, CLAUDIO, BENEDICK, BALTHASAR, DON JOHN, BORACHIO, MARGARET, URSULA, and Others, masked.]

DON PEDRO
Lady, will you walk about with your friend?

Lady, will you walk about with me, your friend?

HERO
So you walk softly and look sweetly and say nothing, I am yours for the walk; and especially when I walk away.

As long as you walk softly and look sweetly and say nothing, I am yours for the walk; and especially when I walk away.

DON PEDRO
With me in your company?

Will I be with you?

HERO
I may say so, when I please.

I might say so, when I please.

DON PEDRO
And when please you to say so?

And what will make it please you to say so?

HERO
When I like your favour;
for God defend the lute should be like the case!

*When I like your attention,
for God defend the lute should be its case!*

DON PEDRO
My visor is Philemon's roof;
within the house is Jove.

*My mask is Philemon's roof;
Jove [the Roman name for Zeus] is inside the house.*

HERO
Why, then, your visor should be thatch'd.

Why, then, your mask should be thatched.

DON PEDRO
Speak low, if you speak love.
[Takes her aside.]

Speak softly, if you speak lovingly.

BALTHAZAR
Well, I would you did like me.

Well, I wish you did like me.

MARGARET
So would not I, for your own sake;
for I have many ill qualities.

*I do not, for your own sake;
for I have many flaws.*

BALTHAZAR
Which is one?

What is one of them?

MARGARET
I say my prayers aloud.

I say my prayers aloud.

BALTHAZAR
I love you the better; the hearers may cry Amen.

That makes me love you more; the hearers may reply, 'Amen.'

MARGARET
God match me with a good dancer!

God match me with a good dancer!

BALTHAZAR
Amen.

Amen.

MARGARET
And God keep him out of my sight when the dance is done! Answer, clerk.

And God get rid of him when the dance is done! Answer me, clerk.

BALTHAZAR
No more words: the clerk is answered.

I have nothing to say: the clerk is answered.

URSULA
I know you well enough: you are Signior Antonio.

I can tell who you are: you are Sir Antonio.

ANTONIO
At a word, I am not.

Really, I'm not.

URSULA
I know you by the waggling of your head.

I know you by how you move your head.

ANTONIO
To tell you true, I counterfeit him.

To tell you the truth, I am pretending to be him.

URSULA
You could never do him so ill-well, unless you were the very man. Here's his dry hand up and down: you are he, you are he.

You could never do such a good job pretending, unless you were the actual man. Here is his dry hand, absolutely the same: you are him, you are him.

ANTONIO
At a word, I am not.

Really, I'm not.

URSULA
Come, come; do you think I do not know you by your excellent wit?
Can virtue hide itself? Go to, mum, you are he: graces will appear, and there's an end.

*Oh, come on; do you think I cannot you by your wittiness?
Can virtue hide itself? Enough, stop protesting, you are him: qualities will appear, and that's the end of it.*

BEATRICE
Will you not tell me who told you so?

Won't you tell me who told you that?

BENEDICK
No, you shall pardon me.

No, you'll have to excuse me.

BEATRICE
Nor will you not tell me who you are?

And won't you tell me who you are?

BENEDICK
Not now.

Not now.

BEATRICE
That I was disdainful, and that I had my good
wit out of the 'Hundred Merry Tales.' Well,
this was Signior Benedick that said so.

*That I am disapproving, and that I took my
witty comments under the 'Hundred Merry
Tales.' Well, this was Sir Benedick who said
so.*

BENEDICK
What's he?

Who's he?

BEATRICE
I am sure you know him well enough.

I'm sure you know him well enough.

BENEDICK
Not I, believe me.

No I don't, believe me

BEATRICE
Did he never make you laugh?

Did he never make you laugh?

BENEDICK
I pray you, what is he?

Please tell me, who is he?

BEATRICE
Why, he is the prince's jester: a very dull fool;
only his gift is in devising impossible slanders:
none but libertines delight in him; and the
commendation is not in his wit, but in his villany;
for he both pleases men and angers them, and
then they laugh at him and beat him. I am sure
he is in the fleet: I would he had boarded me!

*Why, he is the prince's jester: a very boring
fool; only his gift is in coming up with
impossible insults: only immoral men enjoy
his company; and the approval is not in his
wit, but in his badness; for he both pleases
men and angers them, and then they laugh at
him and beat him. I am sure he is present at
the party: I wish he had come to me!*

BENEDICK
When I know the gentleman,
I'll tell him what you say.

*When I know the gentleman,
I'll tell him what you say.*

BEATRICE

Do, do: he'll but break a comparison or two on me; which, peradventure not marked or not laughed at, strikes him into melancholy; and then there's a partridge wing saved, for the fool will eat no supper that night. [Music within.] We must follow the leaders.

Do, do: he'll only make a few insults back at me; which, when they are not noticed or or laughed at, will make him gloomy; and then there's a partridge wing saved, for the fool will eat no supper that night. [Music within.] We must follow the leaders.

BENEDICK
In every good thing.

In every good thing they do.

BEATRICE
Nay, if they lead to any ill, I will leave them at the next turning.

No, if they lead us to anything bad, I will leave them at the next turn.

[Dance. Then exeunt all but DON JOHN, BORACHIO, and CLAUDIO.]

DON JOHN
Sure my brother is amorous on Hero, and hath withdrawn her father to break with him about it. The ladies follow her and but one visor remains.

Surely my brother is in love with Hero, and has spoken privately with her father about it. The ladies follow her and only one mask remains.

BORACHIO
And that is Claudio: I know him by his bearing.

And that is Claudio: I know him by how he walks.

DON JOHN
Are you not Signior Benedick?

Aren't you Sir Benedick?

CLAUDIO
You know me well; I am he.

You know me too well. I am Sir Benedick?

DON JOHN
Signior, you are very near my brother in his love: he is enamoured on Hero; I pray you, dissuade him from her; she is no equal for his birth: you may do the part of an honest man in it.

Sir, you are very dear to my brother: he is enamored with Hero; please, persuade him not to go after her; she is too lowborn for him: you may do the part of an honest man in it.

CLAUDIO
How know you he loves her?

How do you know he loves her?

DON JOHN
I heard him swear his affection.

I heard him promise he loved her.

BORACHIO
So did I too; and he swore he would marry her to-night.

So did I, too; and he promised he would marry her tonight.

DON JOHN
Come, let us to the banquet.

Let us go to the banquet.

[Exeunt DON JOHN and BORACHIO.]

CLAUDIO
Thus answer I in name of Benedick,

I answer in this way under the name of Benedick,

But hear these ill news with the ears of Claudio.

But here this bad news with the ears of Claudio.

'Tis certain so; the prince wooes for himself.
Friendship is constant in all other things
Save in the office and affairs of love:
Herefore all hearts in love use their own tongues;

It is certain; the prince woos for himself.
Friendship is loyal in all other things
Except for in the business of love:
From now on all hearts in love should use their own tongues;

Let every eye negotiate for itself
And trust no agent; for beauty is a witch
Against whose charms faith melteth into blood.

And see for themselves
Trust no one, beauty is a witch
Against whose magic powers faith melts into blood.

This is an accident of hourly proof,

This is an accident of time,

Which I mistrusted not. Farewell, therefore, Hero!

When I was too trusting. Farewell, therefore, Hero!

[Re-enter Benedick.]

BENEDICK
Count Claudio?

Count Claudio?

CLAUDIO
Yea, the same.

Yes, it's me.

BENEDICK
Come, will you go with me?

Will you come with me?

CLAUDIO
Whither?

Where?

BENEDICK
Even to the next willow, about your own business,
count. What fashion will you wear the garland
of? About your neck, like a usurer's chain? or
under your arm, like a lieutenant's scarf?
You must wear it one way, for the prince
hath got your Hero.

To the next willow tree, on your own business, Count. How will you wear the garland? Around your neck, like a banker's chain? Or under your arm, like a lieutenant's scarf? You must wear it one way, for the prince has got your Hero.

CLAUDIO
I wish him joy of her.

I hope he enjoys her.

BENEDICK
Why, that's spoken like an honest drovier: so they sell bullocks. But did you think the prince would have served you thus?

Why, that's spoken like an honest herder: that's how they sell cattle. But did you think the prince would have done this to you?

CLAUDIO
I pray you, leave me.

Please, leave me alone.

BENEDICK
Ho! now you strike like the blind man: 'twas the boy that stole your meat, and you'll beat the post.

Ha! Now you strike out like a blind man: it was the boy that stole your food, and you'll beat the post.

CLAUDIO
If it will not be, I'll leave you.

If you won't leave, I will.

[Exit.]

BENEDICK
Alas! poor hurt fowl. Now will he creep into sedges. But, that my Lady Beatrice should know me, and not know me! The prince's fool! Ha! it may be I go under that title because I am merry. Yea, but so I am apt to do myself wrong; I am not so reputed: it is the base though bitter disposition of Beatrice that puts the world into her person, and so gives me out. Well, I'll be revenged as I may.

Oh dear, the poor wounded bird. Now he will crawl around and mope. But, that my Lady Beatrice should know me, and not know me! The prince's fool! Hah! I might go under that title because of my cheerfulness. Yes, but I am also inclined to do myself wrong; I am not thought of that way: it is the resentment of Beatrice that puts the world into her person, and so gives me out. Well, I'll take what revenge I can.

[Re-enter Don Pedro.]

DON PEDRO
Now, signior, where's the count?
Did you see him?

Now sir where is Claudio?
Did you see him?

BENEDICK
Troth, my lord, I have played the part of Lady Fame. I found him here as melancholy as a lodge in a warren.
I told him, and I think I told him true, that your Grace had got the good will of this young lady; and I offered him my company to a willow tree, either to make him a garland, as being forsaken,

Truthfully, my lord, I have played the part of Fate. I found him here all gloomy.
I told him,
that your Grace had got the good will of this young lady; and I offered him my company to a willow tree, either to make him a garland, as someone who has lost, or to make him a

34

or to bind him up a rod, as being worthy to be whipped.

DON PEDRO
To be whipped! What's his fault?

BENEDICK
The flat transgression of a school-boy, who, being overjoy'd with finding a bird's nest, shows it his companion, and he steals it.

DON PEDRO.
Wilt thou make a trust a transgression? The transgression is in the stealer.

BENEDICK
Yet it had not been amiss the rod had been made, and the garland too; for the garland he might have worn himself, and the rod he might have bestowed on you, who, as I take it, have stolen his bird's nest.

DON PEDRO
I will but teach them to sing, and restore them to the owner.

BENEDICK
If their singing answer your saying, by my faith, you say honestly.

DON PEDRO
The Lady Beatrice hath a quarrel to you: the gentleman that danced with her told her she is much wronged by you.

BENEDICK
O! she misused me past the endurance of a block: an oak but with one green leaf on it, would have answered her: my very visor began to assume life and scold with her. She told me, not thinking I had been myself, that I was the prince's jester, that I was duller than a great thaw; huddling jest upon jest with such impossible conveyance upon me, that I stood like a man at a mark, with a whole army shooting at me. She speaks poniards, and

switch, as being worthy to be whipped.

Beating! What did he do?

The basic error of a schoolboy, who, being overjoyed with finding a bird's nest, shows it to his companion, and his companion steals it.

Will you make it wrong to trust someone? The wrong is in the thief.

Yet it would not have been unsuitable if a switch had been made, and a garland too; for the garland he might have worn himself, and the rod he might have given to you, who, as I understand, have stolen his bird's nest.

I will only teach the birds to sing, and restore them to the owner.

If their singing is the same as your saying, by my faith, you are being honest.

The Lady Beatrice has a quarrel with you: the gentleman that danced with her told her you have much wronged her.

Oh! She abused me more than even a block of wood could endure: an oak with only one green leaf on it would have answered her: my very mask began to come to life and scold her. She told me, not thinking that I had been myself, that I was the prince's jester, that I was more boring than watching ice melt; adding joke upon joke with such an impossible attack of me, that I stood like a man at a

every word stabs: if her breath were as terrible as her terminations, there were no living near her; she would infect to the north star. I would not marry her, though she were endowed with all that Adam had left him before he transgressed: she would have made Hercules have turned spit, yea, and have cleft his club to make the fire too. Come, talk not of her; you shall find her the infernal Ate in good apparel. I would to God some scholar would conjure her, for certainly, while she is here, a man may live as quiet in hell as in a sanctuary; and people sin upon purpose because they would go thither; so indeed, all disquiet, horror and perturbation follow her.

target, with a whole army shooting at me. She speaks with spears, and every word stabs: if her breath was as terrible as her words, nothing could live near her; she would infect everything from here to the North Star. I would not marry her, even if she possessed every possible other good quality. She would have made Hercules commit suicide. Come, do not talk about her; you shall find her a well-dressed demon. I pray to God some scholar will write about her, for certainly, while she is here, a man may live as quietly in hell as in a sanctuary; and people sin on purpose to go there; so indeed, all chaos, horror, and distress follow her.

[Re-enter CLAUDIO, BEATRICE, HERO, and LEONATO.]

DON PEDRO
Look! here she comes.

Look, here she comes!

BENEDICK
Will your Grace command me any service to the world's end? I will go on the slightest errand now to the Antipodes that you can devise to send me on; I will fetch you a toothpicker now from the furthest inch of Asia; bring you the length of Prester John's foot; fetch you a hair off the Great Cham's beard; do you any embassage to the Pygmies, rather than hold three words' conference with this harpy.
You have no employment for me?

Will your Grace command me to do any task for you far away? I will go on the slightest errand now to the Antipodes that you can come up with to send me on; I will fetch you a toothpick from the furthest corner of Asia; bring you the length of Prester John's foot; fetch you a hair off the Great Cham's beard; be an ambassador to the Pygmies, rather than exchange three words with this harpy [a mythological monster with a woman's head and a bird's body]. Do you have anything for me to do?

DON PEDRO
None, but to desire your good company.

Nothing, except to want your company.

BENEDICK
O God, sir, here's a dish I love not:
I cannot endure my Lady Tongue.

*Oh God, sir, here's a dish I hate:
I cannot endure my Lady Tongue.*

[Exit.]

DON PEDRO
Come, lady, come;

Come Lady

you have lost the heart of Signior Benedick.

BEATRICE
Indeed, my lord, he lent it me awhile; and I
gave him use for it, a double heart for a single
one: marry, once before he won it of me with
false dice, therefore your Grace may well say
I have lost it.

DON PEDRO
You have put him down, lady,
you have put him down.

BEATRICE.
So I would not he should do me, my lord, lest
I should prove the mother of fools. I have
brought Count Claudio, whom you sent me to
seek.

DON PEDRO
Why, how now, count! wherefore are you sad?

CLAUDIO
Not sad, my lord.

DON PEDRO
How then? Sick?

CLAUDIO
Neither, my lord.

BEATRICE
The count is neither sad, nor sick, nor merry,
nor well; but civil count, civil as an orange,
and something of that jealous complexion.

DON PEDRO
I' faith, lady, I think your blazon to be true;
though, I'll be sworn, if he be so, his conceit is
false. Here, Claudio, I have wooed in thy name,
and fair Hero is won; I have broke with her
father, and, his good will obtained; name the
day of marriage, and God give thee joy!

LEONATO

You have lost Sir Benedick's heart.

*Indeed, my lord, he lent it to me awhile; and
I exchanged something for it, a double heart
for a single one: by the Virgin Mary, once
before he won it from me through a trick,
therefore your Grace may well say I have lost
it.*

*You've humiliated him lady
and put him down.*

*So I would rather he not do that to me, my
lord, otherwise I might turn out to be the
mother of fools. I have brought Count
Claudio, whom you sent me to look for.*

*Why, what's going on, Count? Why are you
sad?*

I'm not my lord

Sick then?

Neither, my lord.

*The count is neither sad, nor sick, nor
cheerful, nor well; but a polite count, polite
as an orange, and similar to that jealous skin
color.*

*By my faith, lady, I think you are right;
though, I swear, if he is that way, he's acting
under a delusion. Here, Claudio,
I have wooed on your behalf, and beautiful
Hero is won; I have asked permission from
her father, and have gained it; name the day
of marriage, and God give you joy!*

Count, take of me my daughter, and with her my fortunes: his Grace hath made the match, and all grace say Amen to it!

BEATRICE
Speak, Count, 'tis your cue.

CLAUDIO
Silence is the perfectest herald of joy: I were but little happy, if I could say how much. Lady, as you are mine, I am yours: I give away myself for you and dote upon the exchange.

BEATRICE
Speak, cousin; or, if you cannot, stop his mouth with a kiss, and let not him speak neither.

DON PEDRO
In faith, lady, you have a merry heart.

BEATRICE
Yea, my lord; I thank it, poor fool, it keeps on the windy side of care. My cousin tells him in his ear that he is in her heart.

CLAUDIO
And so she doth, cousin.

BEATRICE
Good Lord, for alliance! Thus goes every one to the world but I, and I am sunburnt. I may sit in a corner and cry heigh-ho for a husband!

DON PEDRO
Lady Beatrice, I will get you one.

BEATRICE
I would rather have one of your father's getting. Hath your Grace ne'er a brother like you?

Your father got excellent husbands, if a maid could come by them.

DON PEDRO
Will you have me, lady?

Count, take my daughter, and with her my fortunes: his Grace has made the match, and all grace agrees with it!

Speak, Count, it is your cue.

Silence is the most perfect herald of joy: I would be only a little happy if I were capable of saying how much. Lady, as you are mine, I am yours: I give myself away for you and deeply love the exchange.

Speak, cousin; or, if you cannot, shut him up with a kiss, and keep him from speaking too.

By my faith, lady, you have a cheery heart.

Yes, my lord; I think it, poor fool, it protects me from worries. My cousin tells him in his ear that he is in her heart.

And so she does, cousin.

Good Lord, for marriage! In this way everyone in the world goes but I, and I am sunburned. I may sit in a corner and wail for a husband!

Lady Beatrice, I will get you a husband.

I would rather have one your father got. Does your Grace have a brother like you?

Your father got excellent husbands, if a young woman could come across them.

Will you have me, lady?

BEATRICE
No, my lord, unless I might have another for working days: your Grace is too costly to wear every day. But, I beseech your Grace, pardon me; I was born to speak all mirth and no matter.

No, my lord, unless I might have another for weekdays: your Grace is too costly to wear every day. But, I beg your Grace, please pardon me; I would born to speak nothing but silliness.

DON PEDRO
Your silence most offends me, and to be merry best becomes you; for out of question, you were born in a merry hour.

Your silence most offends me, and to be cheerful shows you at your best; for out of the question, you were born in a merry hour.

BEATRICE
No, sure, my lord, my mother cried; but then there was a star danced, and under that was I born. Cousins, God give you

My mother cried; but then a star danced, and other that I was born. Cousins, God give you joy!

LEONATO
Niece, will you look to those things I told you of?

Niece, will you go take care of those things I mentioned?

BEATRICE
I cry you mercy, uncle. By your Grace's pardon.

Forgive me, uncle. Pardon me, your Grace.

[Exit.]

DON PEDRO
By my troth, a pleasant spirited lady.

Truthfully, a pleasant spirited lady.

LEONATO
There's little of the melancholy element in her, my lord: she is never sad but when she sleeps; and not ever sad then, for I have heard my daughter say, she hath often dreamed of unhappiness and waked herself with laughing.

There is very little gloominess in her, my lord: she is never sad except when she sleeps; and not always sad then, for I have heard my daughter say she has often dreamed of unhappiness and waked herself with laughter.

DON PEDRO
She cannot endure to hear tell of a husband.

She cannot stand to have a husband suggested to her.

LEONATO
O!

Oh,

by no means: she mocks all her wooers out of suit.

by no means: she drives all her wooers away with mocking.

DON PEDRO
She were an excellent wife for Benedick.

She would be an excellent wife for Benedick.

LEONATO

O Lord! my lord, if they were but a week married, they would talk themselves mad.

DON PEDRO
Count Claudio, when mean you to go to church?

CLAUDIO
To-morrow, my lord. Time goes on crutches till love have all his rites.

LEONATO
Not till Monday, my dear son, which is hence a just seven-night; and a time too brief too, to have all things answer my mind.

DON PEDRO
Come, you shake the head at so long a breathing; but, I warrant thee, Claudio, the time shall not go dully by us. I will in the interim undertake one of Hercules' labours, which is, to bring Signior Benedick and the Lady Beatrice into a mountain of affection the one with the other. I would fain have it a match; and I doubt not but to fashion it, if you three will but minister such assistance as I shall give you direction.

LEONATO
My lord, I am for you, though it cost me ten nights' watchings.

CLAUDIO
And I, my lord.

DON PEDRO
And you too, gentle Hero?

HERO
I will do any modest office, my lord, to help my cousin to a good husband.

DON PEDRO
And Benedick is not the unhopefullest husband that I know. Thus far can I praise him; he is of a noble strain, of approved valour, and confirmed honesty. I will teach you how to humour your

Oh Lord! My lord, after only a week of of marriage they would talk themselves crazy.

Count Claudio, when do you mean to have the wedding?

Tomorrow, my lord. Time crawls until love has what it wants.

Not till Monday, my dear son, which is only a week from now; and too brief a time, actually, to get everything done.

Come, you shake your head at such a long wait; but, I promise you, Claudio, the time will not go dully by us. I will in the meantime take up a task worthy of Hercules, which is to bring Sir Benedick and the Lady Beatrice to fall in love with each other. I would like for it to be a match; and I do not doubt that it can can be done, if you three will only give me the help doing as I tell you.

My lord, I am for your cause, even if it costs me ten nights' sleep.

Me to my lord.

And you too, gentle Hero?

I will do any humble work, my lord, to help my cousin get a good husband.

And Benedick is one of the better possible husbands I know. I can praise him in these things: he is a nobleman, known to be brave, and is confirmed as honest. I will teach you

cousin, that she shall fall in love with Benedick; and I, with your two helps, will so practise on Benedick that, in despite of his quick wit and his queasy stomach, he shall fall in love with Beatrice. If we can do this, Cupid is no longer an archer: his glory shall be ours, for we are the only love-gods. Go in with me, and I will tell you my drift.

[Exeunt.]

how to behave towards your cousin, that she shall fall in love with Benedick; and I, with you two helping, will act on Benedick so that, despite his reluctance to marry and his sarcastic nature, he shall fall in love with Beatrice. If we can do this, Cupid is no longer longer an archer: his glory shall be ours, for we will be the only love-gods. Go in with me, and I will tell you my plan.

Scene II

Another room in LEONATO'S house.

[Enter DON JOHN and BORACHIO.]

DON JOHN
It is so; the Count Claudio shall marry
the daughter of Leonato.

It's arranged, Count Claudio will marry Leonato's daughter.

BORACHIO
Yea, my lord; but I can cross it.

Yes, my lord; but I can prevent it.

DON JOHN
Any bar, any cross, any impediment will be
medicinable to me: I am sick in displeasure
to him, and whatsoever comes athwart his
affection ranges evenly with mine. How canst
thou cross this marriage?

Any obstacle, any prevention, any impediment will be like medicine to me: I am sick with displeasure with him, and anything that can stop his affection will have my affection. How can you prevent this marriage?

BORACHIO
Not honestly, my lord; but so covertly that
no dishonesty shall appear in me.

Not honestly, my lord; but so covertly that I will not appear to be dishonest.

DON JOHN
Show me briefly how.

Explain briefly.

BORACHIO
I think I told your lordship, a year since,
how much I am in the favour of Margaret,
the waiting-gentlewoman to Hero.

I think I told your lordship a year ago how much I am beloved by Margaret, Hero's lady-in-waiting.

DON JOHN
I remember.

I remember.

BORACHIO
I can, at any unseasonable instant of the night,
appoint her to look out at her lady's chamber
window.

I can, at any time of the night, ask her to look out at her lady's chamber window.

DON JOHN
What life is in that, to be the death of this
marriage?

What good is that in the destruction of this marriage?

BORACHIO

The poison of that lies in you to temper. Go you to the prince your brother; spare not to tell him, that he hath wronged his honour in marrying the renowned Claudio,--whose estimation do you mightily hold up,--to a contaminated stale, such a one as Hero.

DON JOHN
What proof shall I make of that?

BORACHIO
Proof enough to misuse the prince, to vex Claudio, to undo Hero, and kill Leonato. Look you for any other issue?

DON JOHN
Only to despite them, I will endeavour anything.

BORACHIO
Go then; find me a meet hour to draw Don Pedro and the Count Claudio alone: tell them that you know that Hero loves me; intend a kind of zeal both to the prince and Claudio, as--in love of your brother's honour, who hath made this match, and his friend's reputation, who is thus like to be cozened with the semblance of a maid,--that you have discovered thus. They will scarcely believe this without trial: offer them instances, which shall bear no less likelihood than to see me at her chamber-window, hear me call Margaret Hero, hear Margaret term me Claudio; and bring them to see this the very night before the intended wedding: for in the meantime I will so fashion the matter that Hero shall be absent; and there shall appear such seeming truth of Hero's disloyalty, that jealousy shall be called assurance, and all the preparation overthrown.

DON JOHN
Grow this to what adverse issue it can, I will put it in practice. Be cunning in the working this, and thy fee is a thousand ducats.

BORACHIO

Poisoning it is up to you. Go to the prince your brother; acting as if you are making a confession, that he has wronged his honor in marrying the renowned Claudio – whom you highly respect – to a contaminated slut like Hero.

How can I prove it?

You will have enough proof to upset the prince, distress Claudio, destroy Hero, and be the death of Leonato. Is there anything else you want?

Just to cause them trouble, I will try anything.

Go then; find me a good time to get Don Pedro and the Count Claudio alone: tell them that you know Hero loves me; pretend to be devoted to both the prince and Claudio, as – in love of your brother's honor, who has made this match, and his friend's reputation, who is likely to be tricked into marrying an impure woman – that you have discovered this. They will not believe it without evidence: offer them this proof, where they see me at her chamber-window, hear me call Margaret "Hero", hear Margaret call me "Claudio"; and bring them to see this the the very night before the intended wedding: I will make sure Hero is absent; and there appear such a seeming truth of Hero's disloyalty that jealousy will find confirmation, and all the preparation will be overthrown.

Make this happen; I will put it into practice. Be cunning in bringing this about and I will pay you a thousand ducats.

Be you constant in the accusation,
and my cunning shall not shame me.

*As long as you are consistent
in the accusation my cunning will not fail me.*

DON JOHN
I will presently go learn their day of marriage.

I will now go learn their day of marriage.

[Exeunt.]

Scene III

LEONATO'S Garden.

[Enter Benedick.]

BENEDICK
Boy!

[Enter a Boy.]

BOY
Signior?

BENEDICK
In my chamber-window lies a book;
bring it hither to me in the orchard.

BOY
I am here already, sir.

BENEDICK
I know that; but I would have thee hence, and
here again.
[Exit Boy.]
I do much wonder that one man, seeing how
much another man is a fool when he dedicates
his behaviours to love, will, after he hath laughed
at such shallow follies in others, become the
argument of his own scorn by falling in love: and
such a man is Claudio. I have known, when there
was no music with him but the drum and the fife;
and now had he rather hear the tabor and the pipe:
I have known when he would have walked ten
mile afoot to see a good armour; and now will he
lie ten nights awake, carving the fashion of a new
doublet. He was wont to speak plain and to the
purpose, like an honest man and a soldier; and
now is he turned orthography; his words are a
very fantastical banquet, just so many strange
dishes. May I be so converted, and see with these
eyes? I cannot tell; I think not: I will not be sworn
but love may transform me to an oyster; but I'll
take my oath on it, till he have made an oyster of
me, he shall never make me such a fool.

Boy!

[Enter a Boy.]

Sir?

*In my chamber-window there is a book;
bring it here to me in the orchard.*

I am here already, sir.

*I know that; but I would have you go there,
and come back again.*
[Exit Boy.]
*I do much wonder that one man, seeing how
much another man is a fool when he dedicates
himself to love, will, after he has laughed at
such silliness in others, becomes the very
thing he scorns by falling in love: and such
a man is Claudio. I have known him when
there was no music in him but the drum and
the fife; and now he would rather hear the
tabor and the flute: I have known him when
he would have walked ten miles on food to
see a good set of armor; and now he will lie
awake for ten nights, cutting a nice new suit.
He preferred to speak plainly and straight to
the point, like an honest man and a soldier;
now he uses flowery words, like a fantastical
banquet with so many strange dishes. Will I be
changed like that, and see with those eyes? I
cannot tell; I do not think so: I will not swear
that love will not transform me into an oyster;
but I'll take an oath that, till love makes an*

One woman is fair, yet I am well; another is wise, yet I am well; another virtuous, yet I am well; but till all graces be in one woman, one woman shall not come in my grace. Rich she shall be, that's certain; wise, or I'll none; virtuous, or I'll never cheapen her; fair, or I'll never look on her; mild, or come not near me; noble, or not I for an angel; of good discourse, an excellent musician, and her hair shall be of what colour it please God. Ha! the prince and Monsieur Love! I will hide me in the arbour.

but I'll take an oath that, till love makes an oyster of me, he will never make me such a fool. One woman is beautiful, yet I am unaffected; another is wise, yet I am unaffected; another virtuous, yet I am unaffected; but until all these good qualities are in one woman, not one woman will be high enough quality for me. Rich she shall be, that's certain; wise, or I'll have nothing to do with her; virtuous, or I'll never tough her; beautiful, or I'll never look at her; mild, or I won't let her near me; noble, or she would be out of the question; a good conversationalist, an excellent musician, and her hair can be whatever color pleases God. Hah! The prince and Mister Love! I will hide myself in the tree.
[Withdraws.]

[Withdraws.]

[Enter DON PEDRO, LEONATO, and CLAUDIO, followed by BALTHAZAR and Musicians.]

DON PEDRO
Come, shall we hear this music?

Should we hear the music?

CLAUDIO
Yea, my good lord.
How still the evening is,
As hush'd on purpose to grace harmony!

Yes, my good lord.
How quiet the evening is,
As if hushed on purpose for harmony!

DON PEDRO
See you where Benedick hath hid himself?
himself?

Do you see where Benedick has hidden

CLAUDIO
O! very well, my lord: the music ended,
We'll fit the kid-fox with a penny-worth.

Oh, very well, my lord: once the music ends,
We'll set a trap for the young fox.

DON PEDRO
Come, Balthazar, we'll hear that song again.

Balthazar, let's hear that song again.

BALTHAZAR
O! good my lord, tax not so bad a voice

To slander music any more than once.

Oh! My good lord, please to not trouble such a bad voice
To ruin music any more than once.

DON PEDRO

It is the witness still of excellency,
To put a strange face on his own perfection.
I pray thee, sing, and let me woo no more.

BALTHAZAR
Because you talk of wooing, I will sing;
Since many a wooer doth commence his suit
To her he thinks not worthy; yet he wooes;
Yet will he swear he loves.

DON PEDRO
Nay, pray thee come;
Or if thou wilt hold longer argument,
Do it in notes.

BALTHAZAR
Note this before my notes;
There's not a note of mine that's worth the noting.

DON PEDRO
Why these are very crotchets that he speaks;
Notes, notes, forsooth, and nothing!

[Music.]

BENEDICK
Now, divine air! now is his soul ravished!
Is it not strange that sheep's guts should hale
souls out of men's bodies? Well, a horn for
my money, when all's done.
[Balthazar sings.]
Sigh no more, ladies, sigh no more,
Men were deceivers ever;
One foot in sea, and one on shore,
To one thing constant never.
Then sigh not so,
But let them go,
And be you blithe and bonny,
Converting all your sounds of woe
Into, 'Hey nonny, nonny.'
Sing no more ditties, sing no more
Of dumps so dull and heavy;
The fraud of men was ever so,
Since summer first was leavy.
Then sigh not so,
But let them go,

It is a sign of excellence
To be unable to see its own perfection.
Please, sing, and let me woo no more.

Because you talk of wooing, I will sing;
Since many a wooer begins his courtship
To her he thinks unworthy; yet he woos;
Yet he will swear he loves.

No, please, sing;
Or if you will argue any longer,
Do it in song.

Note this before my notes;
There's not a note of mine that's worth the noting.

Why, this is meaningless talking;
Notes, notes, indeed, and nothing!

Now, divine music! Now his soul is overcome!
Isn't it strange that sheep's guts should bring
joy and draw the souls out of men's bodies?
Well, a horn for me money, when all's done.

Sigh no more, ladies, sigh no more,
Men have always been liars;
One foot in sea, and one on shore,
Never faithful to one thing.
Then do not sigh that way,
But let them go,
And be happy and pretty,
Turning all your sad sounds
Into glad cheers.
Sing no more sad songs, sing no more
Of sorrows so dull and heavy;
The tricks of men have always been this way,
Since summer first began.
Then do not sigh that way,
But let them go,

And be you blithe and bonny,
Converting all your sounds of woe
Into, 'Hey nonny, nonny.'

And be happy and pretty,
Turning all your sad sounds
Into glad cheers.

DON PEDRO
By my troth, a good song.

By the truth, a good song.

BALTHAZAR
And an ill singer, my lord.

And a bad singer, my lord.

DON PEDRO
Ha, no, no, faith;
thou singest well enough for a shift.

Ha, no, no, by my faith;
you sing well enough for the time being.

BENEDICK
[Aside.]
An he had been a dog that should have howled
thus, they would have hanged him; and I pray
God his bad voice bode no mischief. I had as
lief have heard the night-raven, come what
plague could have come after it.

[Aside.]
If he had been a dog that howled that way,
they would have hanged him; and I pray God
his bad voice means no bad luck. I would have
been as willing to have heard the night-raven,
whatever plague could have come after it.

DON PEDRO
Yea, marry; dost thou hear, Balthazar? I pray thee,
get us some excellent music, for to-morrow night
we would have it at the Lady Hero's
chamber-window.

Yes, definitely; do you hear, Balthazar?
Please, get us some excellent music, for
tomorrow night we would like it at the Lady
Hero's bedroom window.

BALTHAZAR
The best I can, my lord.

The best I can, my lord.

DON PEDRO
Do so: farewell.
[Exeunt BALTHAZAR and Musicians.]
Come hither, Leonato: what was it you told
me of to-day, that your niece Beatrice was in
love with Signior Benedick?

Come here, Leonato: what was it that you told
me about today, that your niece Beatrice was
in love with Sir Benedick?

CLAUDIO
O! ay:--
[Aside to DON PEDRO]
Stalk on, stalk on; the fowl sits.

Oh yes!
[Aside to DON PEDRO]
Continue, continue; the bird is listening.

I did never think that lady would have
loved any man.

I did never think that lady would have
loved any man.

LEONATO
No, nor I neither; but most wonderful that she should so dote on Signior Benedick, whom she hath in all outward behaviours seemed ever to abhor.

BENEDICK
[Aside.]
Is't possible? Sits the wind in that corner?

LEONATO
By my troth, my lord, I cannot tell what to think of it but that she loves him with an enraged affection: it is past the infinite of thought.

DON PEDRO
May be she doth but counterfeit.

CLAUDIO
Faith, like enough.

LEONATO
O God! counterfeit! There was never counterfeit of passion came so near the life of passion as she discovers it.

DON PEDRO
Why, what effects of passion shows she?

CLAUDIO
[Aside.]
Bait the hook well: this fish will bite.

LEONATO
What effects, my lord? She will sit you;
[To Claudio.]
You heard my daughter tell you how.

CLAUDIO
She did, indeed.

DON PEDRO
How, how, I pray you? You amaze me:
I would have thought her spirit had been invincible against all assaults of affection.

No, and I didn't think so either; but it is strange that she should have a crush on Sir Benedick, whom she has always acted as though she hated.

[Aside.]
Is it possible? Is that the way the wind is blowing?

Truthfully, my lord, I cannot tell what to think of it except that she loves him with an enraged affection: it is past what I can fathom.

Maybe she is faking it.

By my faith, that is likely.

Oh God! Faking it! There was never pretence of passion that came so near the life of passion as she discovers it

Why what symptoms does she show?

Bait the hook well: and the fish will bite.

What effects, my lord? She will sit in this way – [To Claudio.]
You hear my daughter tell you how.

She did, indeed.

How, how, please tell me! You amaze me: I would have thought her spirit was invincible against any sort of romantic affection.

LEONATO
I would have sworn it had, my lord;
especially against Benedick.

BENEDICK
[Aside]
I should think this a gull, but that the
white-bearded fellow speaks it: knavery cannot,
sure, hide itself in such reverence.

*I would think this was a trick, except the
white-bearded fellow speaks it: trickery
cannot, surely, hide itself behind such a
respectable face.*

CLAUDIO
[Aside.]
He hath ta'en the infection: hold it up.

He has taken the infection: keep going.

DON PEDRO
Hath she made her affection known to Benedick?

*Hath she made her affection known to
Benedick?*

LEONATO
No; and swears she never will: that's her torment.

*No; and swears she never will: that's her
torment.*

CLAUDIO
Tis true, indeed;so your daughter says:
'Shall I,' says she, 'that have so oft encountered
him with scorn, write to him that I love him?'

*It is true, indeed; your daughter says so.
'Shall I,' Beatrice says, 'that has so often met
him with scorn, write to him that I love him?'*

LEONATO
This says she now when she is beginning to write
to him; for she'll be up twenty times a night, and
there will she sit in her smock till she have writ a
sheet of paper: my daughter tells us all.

*She says this now when she is beginning to
write to him; for she'll be up twenty times a
night, and there she will sit in her nightgown
until she has written a sheet of paper: my
daughter tells us all.*

CLAUDIO
Now you talk of a sheet of paper, I remember a
pretty jest your daughter told us of.

*Now you talk of a sheet of paper, I remember
a good joke your daughter told us about.*

LEONATO
O! when she had writ it, and was reading it over,
she found Benedick and Beatrice between the
sheet?

*Oh! When she had written it, and was reading
it over, she found Benedick and Beatrice
between the sheet?*

CLAUDIO
That.

That.

LEONATO
O! she tore the letter into a thousand halfpence;
railed at herself, that she should be so immodest

*Oh! She tore the letter into a thousand pieces;
scolded herself, that she should be so foolish*

to write to one that she knew would flout her:
'I measure him,' says she, 'by my own spirit;
for I should flout him, if he writ to me; yea,
though I love him, I should.'

CLAUDIO
Then down upon her knees she falls, weeps,
sobs, beats her heart, tears her hair, prays,
curses; 'O sweet Benedick! God give me
patience!'

LEONATO
She doth indeed; my daughter says so; and the
ecstasy hath so much overborne her, that my
daughter is sometimes afeard she will do a
desperate outrage to herself. It is very true.

DON PEDRO
It were good that Benedick knew of it by some
other, if she will not discover it.

CLAUDIO
To what end? he would make but a sport of it
and torment the poor lady worse.

DON PEDRO
An he should, it were an alms to hang him. She's
an excellent sweet lady, and, out of all suspicion,
she is virtuous.

CLAUDIO
And she is exceeding wise.

DON PEDRO
In everything but in loving Benedick.

LEONATO
O! my lord, wisdom and blood combating in so
tender a body, we have ten proofs to one that
blood hath the victory. I am sorry for her, as I
have just cause, being her uncle and her guardian.

DON PEDRO
I would she had bestowed this dotage on me; I
would have daffed all other respects and made
her half myself. I pray you, tell Benedick of it,

---

to write to one she knew would reject her:
'I measure him,' she says, 'by my own spirit;
for I would reject him, if he wrote to me;
yes, though I love him, I would.'

Then she falls on her knees, cries, sobs, beats
her chest, tears her hair, prays, curses;
'Oh sweet Benedick! God give me patience!"

She does indeed; my daughter says so; and the
emotions have so much overcome her, that my
daughter is sometimes afraid she will hurt
herself. It is very true.

It would be good if Benedick found out about
it from someone else, if she will not reveal it.

What good would that do? He would only turn
it into a game and torment the poor lady
worse.

If he did, it would be reason enough to hang
him. She's an excellent sweet lady, and, out
of all suspicion, she is virtuous.

And she is exceedingly wise.

In everything but in loving Benedick.

Oh, my lord, wisdom and blood in combat in
in such a delicate body, we have proof that
blood is winning. I am sorry for her, as I have
a good reason, being her uncle and her
guardian.

I wish she had this affection for me; I would
have declined all my other prospects and
married her. Please, tell Benedick about it,

and hear what a' will say.

and here what he will say.

LEONATO
Were it good, think you?

Do you think that would be a good idea?

CLAUDIO
Hero thinks surely she will die; for she says she
will die if he love her not, and she will die ere
she make her love known, and she will die if he
woo her, rather than she will bate one breath of
her accustomed crossness.

*Hero thinks she will surely die; for she says
she will die if he does not love her, and she
will die before she reveals her love, and she
will die if he woos her, rather than take back
one breath of her usual crossness.*

DON PEDRO
She doth well: if she should make tender of her
love, 'tis very possible he'll scorn it; for the man,
--as you know all,--hath a contemptible spirit.

*That is right of her: if she let him know her
love, it is very possible he would reject it;
for the man, -- as you all know, -- has a very
critical personality.*

CLAUDIO
He is a very proper man.

He is a very proper man.

DON PEDRO
He hath indeed a good outward happiness.

He does indeed seem very happy.

CLAUDIO
Fore God, and in my mind, very wise.

To God, and in my mind, very wise.

DON PEDRO
He doth indeed show some sparks that are like wit.

He does indeed show signs of intelligence.

CLAUDIO
And I take him to be valiant.

And I believe him to be brave.

DON PEDRO
As Hector, I assure you: and in the managing of
quarrels you may say he is wise; for either he
avoids them with great discretion, or undertakes
them with a most Christian-like fear.

*As Hector, I assure you: and when dealing
with quarrels you may say he is wise; for
either he discreetly avoids them, or goes about
them with a Christian-like attitude.*

LEONATO
If he do fear God, a' must necessarily keep peace:

*If he does obey God, he must necessarily keep
peace*

if he break the peace, he ought to enter into a
quarrel with fear and trembling.

*if he breaks the peace, he ought to enter
into a quarrel fearfully.*

DON PEDRO

And so will he do; for the man doth fear God,
howsoever it seems not in him by some large jests
he will make. Well, I am sorry for your niece.
Shall we go seek Benedick and tell him of her
love?

CLAUDIO
Never tell him, my lord:
let her wear it out with good counsel.

LEONATO
Nay,
that's impossible: she may wear her heart out first.

DON PEDRO
Well, we will hear further of it by your daughter:
let it cool the while. I love Benedick well, and
I could wish he would modestly examine himself,
to see how much he is unworthy so good a lady.

LEONATO
My lord, will you walk? dinner is ready.

CLAUDIO
[Aside.]
If he do not dote on her upon this,
I will never trust my expectation.

DON PEDRO
[Aside.]
Let there be the same net spread for her; and
that must your daughter and her gentle-woman
carry. The sport will be, when they hold one
an opinion of another's dotage, and no such
matter: that's the scene that I would see, which
will be merely a dumb-show. Let us send her
to call him in to dinner.

[Exeunt DON PEDRO, CLAUDIO, and LEONATO.]

BENEDICK
[Advancing from the arbour.]
This can be no trick: the conference was sadly
borne. They have the truth of this from Hero.
They seem to pity the lady: it seems her
affections have their full bent. Love me! why,

---

*And so will he do; for the man does honor
God, even if it doesn't always seem that way
because of his jokes. Well, I am sorry for your
niece. Shall we go look for Benedick and tell
him of her love?*

*Never tell him, my lord:
let her wear it out with good advice.*

*No,
that's impossible: she may wear her heart out
first.*

*Well, we will hear more about it from your
daughter: leave it be for now. I love Benedick
well, and I wish he would humbly examine
himself, to see how unworthy he is of so good
a lady.*

*Will you come with me, my lord? Dinner is
ready.*

*[Aside.]
If he does not become devoted to her after
this, I will never trust my expectations.*

*[Aside.]
Let the same net be spread for her; and your
daughter and her servant must carry it. The
game will be when each is convinced of the
other's devotion: that's the scene I want to
see, a real show. Let us send her to call
him in to dinner.*

*[Coming from the tree.]
This can be no trick: the conference was a
sad one. They have the truth of this from
Hero. They seem to pity the lady: it seems
her affections are very strong. Love me!*

it must be requited. I hear how I am censured: they say I will bear myself proudly, if I perceive the love come from her;they say too that she will rather die than give any sign of affection. I did never think to marry: I must not seem proud: happy are they that hear their detractions, and can put them to mending. They say the lady is fair: 'tis a truth, I can bear them witness; and virtuous: 'tis so, I cannot reprove it; and wise, but for loving me: by my troth, it is no addition to her wit, nor no great argument of her folly, for I will be horribly in love with her. I may chance have some odd quirks and remnants of wit broken on me, because I have railed so long against marriage; but doth not the appetite alter? A man loves the meat in his youth that he cannot endure in his age. Shall quips and sentences and these paper bullets of the brain awe a man from the career of his humour? No; the world must be peopled. When I said I would die a bachelor, I did not think I should live till I were married. Here comes Beatrice. By this day! she's a fair lady: I do spy some marks of love in her.

Why, I must love her back. I hear how I am criticized: they say I will carry myself proudly, if I see the love comes from her; they say too that she will die rather than give any sign of affection. I never thought to marry: I must not seem proud: it is good for people to be able to hear about their flaws and go about fixing them. They say the lady is beautiful: it is true, I can confirm if; and virtuous: it is true, I cannot disprove it; and wise, except for loving me: truthfully, it is no addition to her intelligence, nor a great sign of foolishness, for I will be horribly in love with her. I may have to deal with some teasing, because I have complained and criticized marriage so much; but doesn't appetite change? A man loves the food when young that he cannot stand when aged. Shall quips and wisecracks prevent a man from following his feelings? No; the world must be populated. When I said I would die a bachelor, I did not think I would live until I was married. Here comes Beatrice. By this day! She's a beautiful lady: I do notice some signs of love in her.

[Enter BEATRICE.]

BEATRICE
Against my will I am sent to bid you come in to dinner.

Against my will I have been sent to tell you to come in to dinner.

BENEDICK
Fair Beatrice, I thank you for your pains.

Lovely Beatrice, I thank you for your pains.

BEATRICE
I took no more pains for those thanks than you take pains to thank me: if it had been painful, I would not have come.

I took no more pains for those thanks than you take pains to thank me: if it had been painful, I would not have come.

BENEDICK
You take pleasure then in the message?
BEATRICE
Yea, just so much as you may take upon a knife's point, and choke a daw withal. You have no stomach, signior: fare you well.

You take pleasure then in the message?

Yes, just as much as you may take in the point of a knife, and choking a bird with it. You have no appetite, sire: farewell.

[Exit.]

BENEDICK
Ha! 'Against my will I am sent to bid you come
in to dinner,' there's a double meaning in that.
'I took no more pains for those thanks than you
took pains to thank me,' that's as much as to say,
Any pains that I take for you is as easy as thanks.
If I do not take pity of her, I am a villain; if I
do not love her, I am a Jew. I will go get her
picture.

[Exit.]

*Ha! 'Against my will I have been sent to tell
you to come in to dinner,' there's a double
meaning in that. 'I took no more pains for
those thanks than your took pains to thank
me,' that's as much to say, 'Any pains that
I take for you is as easy as thanks.' If I do
not pity her, I am a villain; if I do not love her,
I am a miser. I will go get her picture.*

Act III

Scene I

Leonato's Garden.

[Enter HERO, MARGARET, and URSULA.]

HERO
Good Margaret, run thee to the parlour;
There shalt thou find my cousin Beatrice
Proposing with the prince and Claudio:
Whisper her ear, and tell her, I and Ursala
Walk in the orchard, and our whole discourse

Is all of her; say that thou overheard'st us,
And bid her steal into the pleached bower,
Where honey-suckles, ripen'd by the sun,

Forbid the sun to enter; like favourites,
Made proud by princes, that advance their pride
Against that power that bred it.
There will she hide her,
To listen our propose.
This is thy office;
Bear thee well in it and leave us alone.

MARGARET
I'll make her come, I warrant you, presently.

[Exit.]

HERO
Now, Ursula, when Beatrice doth come,
As we do trace this alley up and down,
Our talk must only be of Benedick:
When I do name him, let it be thy part
To praise him more than ever man did merit.

My talk to thee must be how Benedick
Is sick in love with Beatrice: of this matter
Is little Cupid's crafty arrow made,
That only wounds by hearsay.
[Enter BEATRICE, behind.]
Now begin;

Good Margaret, go run to the parlor;
There you shall find my cousin Beatrice
Talking to the prince and Claudio:
Whisper in her ear and tell her Ursala and I
Are walking in the orchard, and our whole
conversation
Is all about her; say that you overheard us,
And tell her to sneak into the tidy grove,
Where honeysuckle flowers, ripened by the
sun,
Forbid the sun to enter; like favorites,
Made proud by princes, that use their pride
Against the power that made it happen.
There she will hide herself,
To listen to our conversation.
This is your job;
Do it well and leave us alone.

I'll make her come, I promise you, in a
moment.

Now, Ursula, when Beatrice comes,
As we walk up and down this path,
We must only talk about Benedick:
When I mention him, let it be your role
To praise him more than any man ever
deserved.
My talk to you must be about how Benedick
Is sick with love for Beatrice: of this matter
Is little Cupid's crafty arrow made,
That only wounds by rumor.

Now begin;

For look where Beatrice, like a lapwing, runs

Close by the ground, to hear our conference.

URSULA

The pleasant'st angling is to see the fish
Cut with her golden oars the silver stream,
And greedily devour the treacherous bait:
So angle we for Beatrice; who even now
Is couched in the woodbine coverture.
Fear you not my part of the dialogue.

HERO

Then go we near her, that her ear lose nothing

Of the false sweet bait that we lay for it.
[They advance to the bower.]
No, truly, Ursula, she is too disdainful;
I know her spirits are as coy and wild
As haggards of the rock.

URSULA

But are you sure
That Benedick loves Beatrice so entirely?

HERO

So says the prince, and my new-trothed lord.

URSULA

And did they bid you tell her of it, madam?

HERO

They did entreat me to acquaint her of it;

But I persuaded them, if they lov'd Benedick,
To wish him wrestle with affection,

And never to let Beatrice know of it.

URSULA

Why did you so?
Doth not the gentleman
Deserve as full as fortunate a bed
As ever Beatrice shall couch upon?

For look where Beatrice, like a lapwing bird, runs
Close by the ground, to hear our conversation.

The most pleasant angling is to see the fish
Cut with her golden fins the silver stream,
And greedily devour the treacherous bait:
So angle we for Beatrice; who even now
Is crouched in the woody cover.
Do not worry about me doing my part of the dialogue.

Then we will go near her, so her ear will lose nothing
Of the lying sweet bait that we set out for it.
[They walk forward to the clump of trees.]
No, truly, Ursula, she is too disapproving;
I know her spirits are as shy and wild
As mountain-dwelling animals.

But are you sure
That Benedick loves Beatrice so entirely?

So says the prince, and my new fiancé.

And did they command you to tell her of it, madam?

They did plead with me to let her know about it;
But I persuaded them, if they loved Benedick,
To wish him to overcome his feelings of affection,
And to never let Beatrice know of them.

Why did you do that?
Does the gentleman not
Deserve fully as a wonderful marriage
As Beatrice could ever be able to make?

HERO
O god of love!
I know he doth deserve
As much as may be yielded to a man;
But nature never fram'd a woman's heart
Of prouder stuff than that of Beatrice;
Disdain and scorn ride sparkling in her eyes,

Misprising what they look on, and her wit
Values itself so highly, that to her
All matter else seems weak.
She cannot love,
Nor take no shape nor project of affection,
She is so self-endear'd.

URSULA
Sure I think so;
And therefore certainly it were not good
She knew his love, lest she make sport at it.

HERO
Why, you speak truth. I never yet saw man,

How wise, how noble, young, how rarely featur'd,

But she would spell him backward: if fair-fac'd,

She would swear the gentleman should be her
sister;
If black, why, Nature, drawing of an antick,

Made a foul blot; if tall, a lance ill-headed;
If low, an agate very vilely cut;
If speaking, why, a vane blown with all winds;

If silent, why, a block moved with none.
 So turns she every man the wrong side out,
And never gives to truth and virtue that
Which simpleness and merit purchaseth.

URSULA
Sure, sure, such carping is not commendable.

HERO
No; not to be so odd, and from all fashions,

Oh Cupid!
I know he does deserve
As much as a man may be able to get;
But nature never framed a woman's heart
Of prouder stuff than Beatrice's'
Disapproval and scorn ride sparkling in her
eyes,
Devaluing what they look upon, and her wit
Values itself so highly, that to her
Everything else seems weak.
She can't love,
Nor take any shape or form of love,
She is so in love with herself.

I surely think so;
And therefore certainly it would not be good
That she knew his love, in case she might
make fun of it.

Why, you speak the truth. I have never yet
seen a man,
No matter now wise, now noble, young, how
handsome,
But that she would drive him away: if
handsome,
She would swear the gentleman should be her
sister;
If dark, why, she would say Nature, drawing a
picture
Blotted the ink; if tall, like a badly made spire;
If short, like a jewel very badly cut;
If speaking, why, a weathervane blown with
all winds;
If silent, why, a block moved by none.
So she gets the wrong image of every man,
And never gives in to the truth and virtue that
Simplicity and merit buys.

Sure, sure, such pickiness is not praiseworthy.

No; not to be so against things, and from all
kinds,

As Beatrice is, cannot be commendable.
But who dare tell her so? If I should speak,
She would mock me into air:
O! she would laugh me
Out of myself, press me to death with wit.
Therefore let Benedick, like cover'd fire,
Consume away in sighs, waste inwardly:
It were a better death than die with mocks,

Which is as bad as die with tickling.

URSULA
Yet tell her of it: hear what she will say.

HERO
No; rather I will go to Benedick,
And counsel him to fight against his passion.
And, truly, I'll devise some honest slanders

To stain my cousin with.
One doth not know
How much an ill word may empoison liking.

URSULA
O! do not do your cousin such a wrong.
She cannot be so much without true judgment,

-- Having so swift and excellent a wit
As she is priz'd to have,--as to refuse
So rare a gentleman as Signior Benedick.

HERO
He is the only man of Italy,
Always excepted my dear Claudio.

URSULA
I pray you, be not angry with me, madam,
Speaking my fancy: Signior Benedick,
For shape, for bearing, argument and valour,

Goes foremost in report through Italy.

HERO
Indeed, he hath an excellent good name.

URSULA

As Beatrice is, cannot be praiseworthy.
But who would dare tell her so? If I spoke,
She would tease me endlessly:
Oh! She would laugh me
Out of myself, squeeze me to death with wit.
Therefore let Benedick, like a covered flame,
Fade away in sighs, waste away inwardly:
It would be a better death than to die of mockery,
Whish is as bad as to die from being tickled.

Still tell her about it: hear what she will say.

No; instead I will go to Benedick,
And advise him to fight against his passion.
And, truly, I'll come up with some honest insults
To make my cousin less appealing.
One does not know
How much an unkind word may poison liking.

Oh! Do not do your cousin such a wrong.
She cannot be so much without good judgment,
-- Being so clever and quick-witted
As she is proud to be – as to refuse
Such a rare gentleman as Sir Benedick.

He is the best man in Italy,
Except my dear Claudio, of course.

Please, do not be angry with me, madam,
Sharing my opinion: Sir Benedick,
For appearance, for behavior, cleverness, and courage,
Is the first man in everything throughout Italy.

Indeed, he has an excellent reputation.

His excellence did earn it, ere he had it.
When are you married, madam?

HERO.
Why, every day, to-morrow.
Come, go in: I'll show thee some attires,
and have thy counsel
Which is the best to furnish me to-morrow.

URSULA
She's lim'd, I warrant you: we have caught her,
madam.

HERO
If it prove so, then loving goes by haps:

Some Cupid kills with arrows, some with traps.

[Exeunt HERO and URSULA.]

BEATRICE
[Advancing.]
What fire is in mine ears?
Can this be true?
Stand I condemn'd for pride and scorn so much?

Contempt, farewell! and maiden pride, adieu!

No glory lives behind the back of such.
And, Benedick, love on; I will requite thee,

Taming my wild heart to thy loving hand:
If thou dost love, my kindness shall incite thee
To bind our loves up in a holy band;
For others say thou dost deserve, and I
Believe it better than reportingly.

[Exit.]

His excellence did earn it, before he had it.
When will you be married, madam?

Why, tomorrow.
Come, go in: I'll show you some clothes,
and get your advice
Which would be the best for me to wear
tomorrow.

She is caught, I believe, madam.

If it turns out that way, than loving goes my
circumstance:
Some Cupid kills with arrows, some with
traps.

What fire is in my ears?
Can this be true?
Do I stand so much condemned for pride and
scorn?
Farewell, contempt! And goodbye maiden
pride!
No glory lives behind either of them.
And, Benedick, love on; I will love you in
return,
Taming my wild heart to your loving hand:
If you do love, my kindness shall bring you
To tie our loves together in a holy ring;
For others say you do deserve, and I
Believe it more than they think I do.

Scene II

A Room in LEONATO'S House.

[Enter DON PEDRO, CLAUDIO, BENEDICK, and LEONATO.]

DON PEDRO
I do but stay till your marriage be consummate, and then go I toward Arragon.

I will only stay until your marriage is accomplished, and then I will go to Arragon.

CLAUDIO
I'll bring you thither, my lord, if you'll vouchsafe me.

I'll take you there, my lord, if you wish me to.

DON PEDRO
Nay, that would be as great a soil in the new gloss of your marriage, as to show a child his new coat and forbid him to wear it. I will only be bold with Benedick for his company; for, from the crown of his head to the sole of his foot, he is all mirth; he hath twice or thrice cut Cupid's bowstring, and the little hangman dare not shoot at him. He hath a heart as sound as a bell, and his tongue is the clapper; for what his heart thinks his tongue speaks.

No, that would be as large a stain on the new gloss of your marriage as to show a child his new coat and forbid him to wear it. I will only request Benedick for his company; for, from the top of his head to the sole of his foot, he is all amusement; he has two or three times times cut Cupid's bowstring, and the little hangman does not dare shoot at him. He has a heart as strong as a bell, and his tongue is the clapper; for what his heart thinks his tongue speaks.

BENEDICK
Gallants, I am not as I have been.

My friends, I am not the same as I was.

LEONATO
So say I: methinks you are sadder.

I agree: you seem sadder.

CLAUDIO
I hope he be in love.

I hope he is in love.

DON PEDRO
Hang him, truant! there's no true drop of blood in him, to be truly touched with love. If he be sad, he wants money.

Hang him, the no-show! There's no true drop of blood in him, to be truly touched with love. If he is sad, he wants money.

BENEDICK
I have the tooth-ache.

I have a toothache.

DON PEDRO

Draw it.

Pull it out.

BENEDICK
Hang it.

Tie it up.

CLAUDIO
You must hang it first, and draw it afterwards.

You must tie it up first, and pull it out afterwards.

DON PEDRO
What! sigh for the tooth-ache?

What, you're all worked up about a toothache?

LEONATO
Where is but a humour or a worm?

Which is only a temporary illness?

BENEDICK
Well, every one can master a grief but he that has it.

Well, it's easy to overcome a trouble until you have it.

CLAUDIO
Yet say I, he is in love.

I say he is in love.

DON PEDRO
There is no appearance of fancy in him, unless it be a fancy that he hath to strange disguises; as to be a Dutchman to-day, a Frenchman to-morrow; or in the shape of two countries at once, as a German from the waist downward, all slops, and a Spaniard from the hip upward, no doublet. Unless he have a fancy to this foolery, as it appears he hath, he is no fool for fancy, as you would have it appear he is.

There is no appearance of fancifulness in him, unless it is a fancifulness that he has to strange disguises; such as to be a Dutchman today, a Frenchman tomorrow; or in the shape of two countries at once, as a German from the waist downward, all sloppy, and a Spaniard from the hip upward, no doublet. Unless he has a fancy to this foolery, as it appears he has, he is no fool for fancy, as you would have it appear he is.

CLAUDIO
If he be not in love with some woman, there is no believing old signs: a' brushes his hat a mornings; what should that bode?

If he is not in love with some woman, there is no reason to believe old signs: if he brushes his hat in the mornings, what does that mean?

DON PEDRO
Hath any man seen him at the barber's?

Has any man seen him at the barber's?

CLAUDIO
No, but the barber's man hath been seen with him; and the old ornament of his cheek hath already stuffed tennis-balls.

No, but the barber's assistant has been seen with him; and the hair that used to decorate his face is now stuffing tennis balls.

LEONATO

Indeed he looks younger than he did,
by the loss of a beard.

*Indeed, he looks younger than he did,
now that he has no beard.*

DON PEDRO
Nay, a' rubs himself with civet:
can you smell him out by that?

*Now, if he rubs himself with cologne,
can you smell him out by that?*

CLAUDIO
That's as much as to say the sweet youth's in love.

*That's as much as to say the sweet youth's in
love.*

DON PEDRO
The greatest note of it is his melancholy.

The most obvious sign of it is his melancholy.

CLAUDIO
And when was he wont to wash his face?

*And since when has he had a tendency to
wash his face?*

DON PEDRO
Yea, or to paint himself? for the which,
I hear what they say of him.

*Yes, or to decorate himself? For I have hear
they say he does.*

CLAUDIO
Nay, but his jesting spirit; which is now crept
into a lute-string, and new-governed by stops.

*No, only his jesting spirit; which has now
crept into a lute-string, and is newly
controlled by holes.*

DON PEDRO
Indeed, that tells a heavy tale for him.
Conclude, conclude he is in love.

*Indeed, the evidence is strong.
Conclude, conclude he is in love.*

CLAUDIO
Nay, but I know who loves him.

No, but I know who loves him.

DON PEDRO
That would I know too:
I warrant, one that knows him not.

*I know that too:
I figure someone who does not know him.*

CLAUDIO
Yes, and his ill conditions; and in despite of all,
dies for him.

*Yes, and his flaws; and despite all of it, dies
for him.*

DON PEDRO
She shall be buried with her face upwards.

She will be buried with her facing upwards.

BENEDICK
Yet is this no charm for the tooth-ache.
Old signior, walk aside with me:
I have studied eight or nine wise words to

*Yet this is no cure for a toothache.
Old sir, walk aside with me:
I have studied eight or nine wise words to*

speak to you, which these hobby-horses must not hear.

speak to you, which these jokesters must not hear.

[Exeunt BENEDICK and LEONATO.]

DON PEDRO
For my life, to break with him about Beatrice.

By my life, he intends to ask for Beatrice's hand.

CLAUDIO
'Tis even so. Hero and Margaret have by this played their parts with Beatrice, and then the two bears will not bite one another when they meet.

It is so. Hero and Margaret have by this time played their parts with Beatrice, and then the two bears will not bite one another when they meet.

[Enter DON JOHN.]

DON JOHN
My lord and brother, God save you!

My lord and brother, God save you!

DON PEDRO
Good den, brother.

Hello, brother.

DON JOHN
If your leisure served, I would speak with you.

If you have the time, I would like to speak with you.

DON PEDRO
In private?

In private?

DON JOHN
If it please you; yet Count Claudio may hear, for what I would speak of concerns him.

If it pleases you; yet Count Claudio may hear, for what I wish to speak of involves him.

DON PEDRO
What's the matter?

What's the matter?

DON JOHN
[To CLAUDIO.]
Means your lordship to be married to-morrow?

Does your lordship mean to be married tomorrow?

DON PEDRO
You know he does.

You know he does.

DON JOHN
I know not that, when he knows what I know.

I don't know about that, when he knows what I know.

CLAUDIO

If there be any impediment,
I pray you discover it.

If there is any obstacle, please reveal it.

DON JOHN
You may think I love you not: let that appear
hereafter, and aim better at me by that I now
will manifest. For my brother, I think he holds
you well, and in dearness of heart hath holp to
effect your ensuing marriage; surely suit ill-spent
and labour ill bestowed!

*You may think I dislike you: let that prove
wrong from now on, and think better of me
by what I will share with you now. For my
brother, I think he holds you in high esteem,
and in his fondness has helped to bring about
your ensuing marriage; surely a waste of time
and terrible gift!*

DON PEDRO
Why, what's the matter?

Why, what's the matter?

DON JOHN
I came hither to tell you; and circumstances
shortened,--for she has been too long a talking
of,--the lady is disloyal.

*I came here to tell you; and to put it briefly, --
for we have discussed her for too long
already, -- the lady is disloyal.*

CLAUDIO.
Who, Hero?

Who, Hero?

DON JOHN
Even she:
Leonato's Hero, your Hero, every man's Hero.

*Even she:
Leonato's Hero, your Hero, every man's Hero.*

CLAUDIO
Disloyal?

Disloyal?

DON JOHN
The word's too good to paint out her wickedness;
I could say, she were worse: think you of a
worse title, and I will fit her to it. Wonder not till
further warrant: go but with me to-night, you
shall see her chamber-window entered, even the
night before her wedding-day: if you love her
then, to-morrow wed her; but it would better
fit your honour to change your mind.

*The word's too good to describe her
wickedness; I could say she was worse: you
think of a worse title, and I will fit her to it.
Do not wonder until there is further reason:
just go with me tonight, you shall see her
chamber-window entered, even the night
before her wedding day: if you love her then,
marry her tomorrow; but it would better fit
your honor to change your mind.*

CLAUDIO
May this be so?

Could this be true?

DON PEDRO
I will not think it.

I won't consider it.

DON JOHN

If you dare not trust that you see, confess not that you know. If you will follow me, I will show you enough; and when you have seen more and heard more, proceed accordingly.

CLAUDIO
If I see anything to-night why I should not marry her to-morrow, in the congregation, where I should wed, there will I shame her.

DON PEDRO
And, as I wooed for thee to obtain her,
I will join with thee to disgrace her.

DON JOHN
I will disparage her no farther till you are my witnesses: bear it coldly but till midnight, and let the issue show itself.

DON PEDRO
O day untowardly turned!

CLAUDIO
O mischief strangely thwarting!

DON JOHN
O plague right well prevented!
So will you say when you have seen the sequel.

[Exeunt.]

If you do not dare trust what you see, do not not confess that you know. If you will follow me, I will show you enough; and when you have seen more and heard more, proceed accordingly.

If I see anything tonight that shows why I should not marry her tomorrow, in the congregation, where I should marry, I will shame her there.

*And as I helped you get her,
I will join with you to disgrace her.*

I will criticize her no further until you are my witnesses: bear it patiently only till midnight, and let the issue prove itself.

Oh day turned unlucky!

Oh mischief strangely ruining!

*Oh terrible fate right well prevented!
That is what you will say when you have seen the second part.*

Scene III

A Street.

[Enter DOGBERRY and VERGES, with the Watch.]

DOGBERRY
Are you good men and true?

Are you good and loyal men?

VERGES
Yea, or else it were pity but they should suffer
salvation, body and soul.

*Yes, or else it would be a pity that they would
suffer salvation [he means damnation], body
and soul.*

DOGBERRY
Nay, that were a punishment too good for them,
if they should have any allegiance in them,
being chosen for the prince's watch.

*No, that would be a punishment to good for
them, if they have any allegiance in them,
being chosen as the prince's guards.*

VERGES
Well, give them their charge, neighbour Dogberry.

*Well, assign them their tasks, neighbor
Dogberry.*

DOGBERRY
First, who think you the most desartless man to
be constable?

*First, who do you think is the best man to be
the constable?*

FIRST WATCH
Hugh Oatcake, sir, or George Seacoal;
for they can write and read.

*Hugh Oatcake, sir, or George Seacoal;
or they can write and read.*

DOGBERRY
Come hither, neighbour Seacoal. God hath
blessed you with a good name: to be a
well-favoured man is the gift of fortune; but to
write and read comes by nature.

*Come here, neighbor Seacoal. God has
blessed you with a good reputation: to be a
well-liked man is the gift of fortune; but to
write and read comes by nature.*

SECOND WATCH
Both which, Master Constable,--

Both which, Master Constable,--

DOGBERRY
You have: I knew it would be your answer.
Well, for your favour, sir, why, give God thanks,
and make no boast of it; and for your writing and
reading, let that appear when there is no need of
such vanity.
You are thought here to be the most senseless

*You have: I knew it would be your answer.
Well, for your being liked, sir, why, give God
thanks, and do not boast about it; and as for
your writing and reading, let that appear
when there is no need of such vanity.
You are thought here to be the most senseless*

and fit man for the constable of the watch;
therefore bear you the lanthorn. This is your
charge: you shall comprehend all vagrom men;
you are to bid any man stand, in the prince's name.

SECOND WATCH
How, if a' will not stand?

DOGBERRY
Why, then, take no note of him, but let him go;
and presently call the rest of the watch together,
and thank God you are rid of a knave.

VERGES
If he will not stand when he is bidden,
he is none of the prince's subjects.

DOGBERRY
True, and they are to meddle with none but the
prince's subjects. You shall also make no noise

in the streets: for, for the watch to babble and
to talk is most tolerable and not to be endured.

SECOND WATCH
We will rather sleep than talk:
we know what belongs to a watch.

DOGBERRY
Why, you speak like an ancient and most
quiet watchman, for I cannot see how sleeping
should offend; only have a care that your bills
be not stolen. Well, you are to call at all the
alehouses, and bid those that are drunk get them
to bed.

SECOND WATCH
How if they will not?

DOGBERRY
Why then, let them alone till they are sober:
if they make you not then the better answer,
you may say they are not the men you took
them for.

SECOND WATCH

*and fit man to be the constable of the guards;
therefore, carry the lantern. This is your
charge: you shall notice all vagrant men; you
are to tell any man to stand, in the prince's
name.*

How, if he will not stand?

*Why, then, take no note of him, but let him go;
and soon after that call the rest of the guards
together, and thank God you have gotten rid
of a scoundrel.*

*If he will not stand when he is told to,
he is not one of the prince's subjects.*

*True, and they are to meddle with none but the
prince's subjects. You shall also make no
noise
in the streets: for, for the watch to babble and
to talk is most tolerable and not to be endured.*

*We will rather sleep than talk:
we know what belongs to a watch.*

*Why, you speak like an old-fashioned and
most quiet watchman, for I cannot see how
sleeping should offend; only be careful that no
one steals your money. Well, you are to call at
all the alehouses, and tell those that are drunk
to get to bed.*

And what is they won't?

*Why then, leave them alone until they are
sober: if they do not then give a better answer,
you may say they are not the men you took
them for.*

Well, sir.

Good, sir.

DOGBERRY
If you meet a thief, you may suspect him, by
virtue of your office, to be no true man; and,
for such kind of men, the less you meddle or
make with them, why, the more is for your honesty.

*If you meet a thief, you may suspect him,
based on your position, to be no loyal man;
and, for such men, the less you deal with them,
why, the more of your honesty is left.*

SECOND WATCH
If we know him to be a thief,
shall we not lay hands on him?

*If we know him to be a thief,
shouldn't we capture him?*

DOGBERRY
Truly, by your office, you may; but I think they
that touch pitch will be defiled. The most peaceable
way for you, if you do take a thief, is to let him
show himself what he is and steal out of your
company.

*Truly, by your position, you man; but I think
they that touch tar will be made unclean. The
most peaceful way for you, if you do take a
thief, is to let him show himself as what he is
and steal away from your company.*

VERGES
You have been always called a merciful man,
partner.

*You have been always called a merciful man,
partner.*

DOGBERRY
Truly, I would not hang a dog by my will,
much more a man who hath any honesty in him.

*Truly, I would not hang a dog by my own
decision, and much more a man who has any
honesty in him.*

VERGES
If you hear a child cry in the night, you must call
to the nurse and bid her still it.

*If you hear a child cry in the night, you must
call to the nanny and tell her to quiet it.*

SECOND WATCH
How if the nurse be asleep and will not hear us?

*What is the nurse is asleep and doesn't hear
us?*

DOGBERRY
Why then, depart in peace, and let the child wake
her with crying; for the ewe that will not hear her
lamb when it baes, will never answer a calf when
he bleats.

*Why then, go in peace, and let the child wake
her with crying; for the female sheep that will
not hear her lamb with it bleats will never
answer a calf when he moos.*

VERGES
'Tis very true.

It is very true.

DOGBERRY
This is the end of the charge. You constable,
are to present the prince's own person: if you

*That is the last of your duties. You, constable,
are to present the prince's own person: if you*

meet the prince in the night, you may stay him.

VERGES
Nay, by'r lady, that I think, a' cannot.

DOGBERRY
Five shillings to one on't, with any man that knows the statutes, he may stay him: marry, not without the prince be willing; for, indeed, the watch ought to offend no man, and it is an offence to stay a man against his will.

VERGES
By'r lady, I think it be so.

DOGBERRY
Ha, ah, ha! Well, masters, good night: an there be any matter of weight chances, call up me: keep your fellows' counsels and your own, and good night. Come, neighbour.

SECOND WATCH
Well, masters, we hear our charge: let us go sit here upon the church-bench till two, and then all to bed.

DOGBERRY
One word more, honest neighbours. I pray you, watch about Signior Leonato's door; for the wedding being there to-morrow, there is a great coil to-night. Adieu; be vigitant, I beseech you.

[Exeunt DOGBERRY and VERGES.]

[Enter BORACHIO and CONRADE.]

BORACHIO
What, Conrade!

WATCH
[Aside.]
Peace! stir not.

BORACHIO
Conrade, I say!
CONRADE

meet the prince in the night, you may stop him.

No, by your leave, I think he cannot.

Five shillings to one on it, with any man that knows the rules, he may stop him: but not without the prince's willingness; for, indeed, the watch should not offend anyone, and it is an offence to stop a man against his will.

By your leave, I think it is so.

Ha, ah, ha! Well, gentlemen, good night: and if anything important happens, call me up: keep your fellows' advice and your own, and good night. Come, neighbor.

Well, gentlemen, we hear our commands: let us go sit here upon the church bench until two, and then we will all go to bed.

One more word, honest neighbors. Please, watch around Sir Leonato's door; since the wedding will be there tomorrow, it is very important tonight. Adieu, be [he mispronounces "vigilant"], I beg you.

What, Conrade!

[Aside.]
Peace! Do not move.

Conrade, I say!

Here, man. I am at thy elbow.

Here, man. I am at your elbow.

BORACHIO
Mass, and my elbow itched;
I thought there would a scab follow.

My, and my elbow itched;
I thought I was getting a scab.

CONRADE
I will owe thee an answer for that;
and now forward with thy tale.

I will answer you for that;
and now go on with your story.

BORACHIO
Stand thee close then under this penthouse,
for it drizzles rain, and I will, like a true drunkard,
utter all to thee.

You stand close then under this penthouse,
for it is drizzling rain, and I will, like a true
drunk man, tell you everything.

WATCH
[Aside.]
Some treason, masters; yet stand close.

[Aside.]
Some betrayal, gentlemen; you should still
stand close by.

BORACHIO
Therefore know, I have earned of Don John a
thousand ducats.

Therefore, know that I have earned from Don
John a thousand ducats.

CONRADE
Is it possible that any villany should be so dear?

Is it possible that any villainy should be so
expensive?

BORACHIO
Thou shouldst rather ask if it were possible any
villany should be so rich; for when rich villains
have need of poor ones, poor ones may make
what price they will.

You should instead ask if it was possible for
any villainy to be so rich; for when rich
villains need poor ones, poor ones may
demand whatever price they wish.

CONRADE
I wonder at it.

I still doubt it.

BORACHIO
That shows thou art unconfirmed. Thou knowest
that the fashion of a doublet, or a hat, or a cloak,
is nothing to a man.

That shows you are unenlightened. You know
that the fashion of a doublet, or a hat, or a
cloak, is nothing to a man.

CONRADE
Yes, it is apparel.

Yes, it is clothing.

BORACHIO
I mean, the fashion.

I mean, the fashion.

CONRADE
Yes, the fashion is the fashion.

Yes, the fashion is the fashion.

BORACHIO
Tush! I may as well say the fool's the fool.
But seest thou not what a deformed thief this
fashion is?

Pshaw! I might as well say the fool's the fool.
But don't you see what a deformed thief this
fashion is?

WATCH
[Aside.]
I know that Deformed; a' bas been a vile thief this
seven years; a' goes up and down like a gentleman:
I remember his name.

[Aside.]
I know that Deformed; he has been a terrible
thief these seven years; he goes up and down
like a nobleman: I remember his name.

BORACHIO
Didst thou not hear somebody?

Did you not hear somebody?

CONRADE
No: 'twas the vane on the house.

No: it was the weathervane on the house.

BORACHIO
Seest thou not, I say, what a deformed thief this
fashion is? how giddily he turns about all the hot
bloods between fourteen and five-and-thirty?
sometime fashioning them like Pharaoh's soldiers
in the reechy painting; sometime like god Bel's
priests in the old church-window; sometime like
the shaven Hercules in the smirched worm-eaten
tapestry, where his codpiece seems as massy as
his club?

Do you not see, I say, what a deformed thief
this fashion is? How giddily he spins around
all the hot-blooded young men between
fourteen and thirty-five? Sometimes shaping
them like Pharaoh's soldiers in a painting;
sometimes like the god Bel's priests in the
church window; sometimes like the shaved
Hercules in the stained worm-eaten tapestry,
where his codpiece seems as massive as his
club?

CONRADE
All this I see, and I see that the fashion wears out
more apparel than the man. But art not thou thyself
giddy with the fashion too, that thou hast shifted
out of thy tale into telling me of the fashion?

I see all this, and I see that fashion wears out
out more clothing than the man. But are you
not yourself giddy with the fashion too, that
you have gotten sidetracked out of your story
into telling me about fashion?

BORACHIO
Not so neither; but know, that I have to-night
wooed Margaret, the Lady Hero's gentlewoman,
by the name of Hero: she leans me out at her
mistress' chamber-window, bids me a thousand
times good night,--I tell this tale vilely:--I should
first tell thee how the prince, Claudio,
and my master, planted and placed and possessed
by my master Don John, saw afar off in the

Oh, that's not true; but know that I have
tonight wooed Margaret, the Lady Hero's
personal attendant, by the name of Hero:
she leans out at me at her mistress' bedroom
window, tells me goodnight a thousand times,
-- I am telling this tale badly –
I should first tell you how the prince, Claudio,
and my master, planted and placed and

orchard this amiable encounter.

CONRADE
And thought they Margaret was Hero?

BORACHIO
Two of them did, the prince and Claudio; but the devil my master, knew she was Margaret; and partly by his oaths, which first possessed them, partly by the dark night, which did deceive them, but chiefly by my villany, which did confirm any slander that Don John had made, away went Claudio enraged; swore he would meet her, as he was appointed, next morning at the temple, and there, before the whole congregation, shame her with what he saw o'er night, and send her home again without a husband.

FIRST WATCH
We charge you in the prince's name, stand!

SECOND WATCH
Call up the right Master Constable. We have here recovered the most dangerous piece of lechery that ever was known in the commonwealth.

FIRST WATCH
And one Deformed is one of them: I know him, a' wears a lock.

CONRADE
Masters, masters!

SECOND WATCH
You'll be made bring Deformed forth, I warrant you.

CONRADE
Masters,--

FIRST WATCH
Never speak:
we charge you let us obey you to go with us.

BORACHIO

possessed by my master Don John, saw far away in the orchard this friendly meeting.

And thought they Margaret was Hero?

Two of them did, the prince and Claudio; but the devil, my master, knew she was Margaret; and partly by his promises, which first possessed them, partly by the dark night, which did deceive them, but most of ally by my villainy, which confirmed the false accusation that Don John had made, Claudio went away angry; swore he would meet her, as he was appointed, next morning at the church, and there, in front of the whole congregation, shame her with what he saw the previous night, and send her home again without a husband.

We command you in the prince's name: stop!

Call up the good Master Constable. We have here discovered the most dangerous piece of wickedness that was ever known in the commonwealth.

And one Deformed is one of them: I know him, he wears a lock.

Gentlemen, gentlemen!

You'll be required to bring Deformed forward, I predict.

Gentlemen, --

*Quiet:
we command you to go with us.*

We are like to prove a goodly commodity, being taken up of these men's bills.

CONRADE
A commodity in question, I warrant you. Come, we'll obey you.

[Exeunt.]

We are likely to turn out to be a valuable resource, being taken up with these men's bills.

A resource in question, I predict. Come, we'll obey you.

Scene IV

A Room in LEONATO'S House.

[Enter HERO, MARGARET, and URSULA.]

HERO
Good Ursula, wake my cousin Beatrice,
and desire her to rise.

*Good Ursula; wake my cousin Beatrice,
and ask her to get up.*

URSULA
I will, lady.

I will, lady.

HERO
And bid her come hither.

And tell her to come here.

URSULA
Well.

Okay.

[Exit.]

MARGARET
Troth, I think your other rabato were better.

*Truthfully, I think your other rabato would be
better.*

HERO
No, pray thee, good Meg, I'll wear this.

No, please, good Meg, I'll wear this.

MARGARET
By my troth's not so good;
and I warrant your cousin will say so.

*By the truth it's not as good;
and I predict your cousin will say so.*

HERO
My cousin 's a fool, and thou art another:
I'll wear none but this.

*My cousin 's a fool, and thou art another:
I'll wear none other than this.*

MARGARET
I like the new tire within excellently, if the hair
were a thought browner; and your gown 's a
most rare fashion, i' faith. I saw the Duchess
of Milan's gown that they praise so.

*I like the new clothes inside excellently, if the
hair was a shade browner; and your gown is
the latest fashion, by my faith. I saw the
Duchess of Milan's gown that they praise in
that way.*

HERO
O! that exceeds, they say.

Oh! That's excessive, they say.

MARGARET

76

By my troth 's but a night-gown in respect of yours: cloth o' gold, and cuts, and laced with silver, set with pearls, down sleeves, side sleeves, and skirts round, underborne with a blush tinsel; but for a fine, quaint, graceful, and excellent fashion, yours is worth ten on't.

HERO
God give me joy to wear it!
for my heart is exceeding heavy.

MARGARET
'Twill be heavier soon by the weight of a man.

HERO
Fie upon thee! art not ashamed?

MARGARET
Of what, lady? of speaking honourably? is not marriage honourable in a beggar? Is not your lord honourable without marriage? I think you would have me say, 'saving your reverence, a husband:' an bad thinking do not wrest true speaking, I'll offend nobody. Is there any harm in 'the heavier for a husband'? None, I think, an it be the right husband and the right wife; otherwise 'tis light, and not heavy: ask my Lady Beatrice else; here she comes.

[Enter BEATRICE.]

HERO
Good morrow, coz.

BEATRICE
Good morrow, sweet Hero.

HERO
Why, how now? do you speak in the sick tune?

BEATRICE
I am out of all other tune, methinks.

MARGARET
Clap's into 'Light o' love'; that goes without a burden: do you sing it, and I'll dance it.

By the truth, it's only a nightgown when compared to yours: gold cloth, and cuts, an laced with silver, set with pearls, down sleeves, side sleeves, and round skirts, trimmed underneath with pink tinsel; but for a fine, quaint, graceful, and excellent fashion, yours is worth ten of it.

God give me joy to wear it!
For my heart is exceedingly heavy.

It will soon be heavier by the weight of a man.

Darn you! Are you not ashamed?

Of what, lady? Of speaking honorably? Is not marriage honorable in a beggar? Is not your fiancé honorable without marriage? I think you want me to say, 'saving your reverence, a husband:' since bad thinking does not stop true speaking, I'll offend nobody. Is there any harm in 'the heavier for a husband'? None, I think, unless it be the right husband and the right wife; otherwise it is light, and not heavy: ask my Lady Beatrice as well; here she comes.

Good morning, cousin.

Good morning, sweet Hero.

Why, what's going on? Do you speak in a sickly way?

I am all out of all other tune, I think.

Clap us into 'Light of Love'; that doesn't have a chorus: you sing it, and I'll dance it.

BEATRICE
Ye, light o' love with your heels! then, if your husband have stables enough, you'll see he shall lack no barnes.

You, light of love with your heels! Then, if your husband has enough stables, you'll see he'll have no lack of foals.

MARGARET
O illegitimate construction!
I scorn that with my heels.

Oh false accusation!
I scorn that with my heels.

BEATRICE
'Tis almost five o'clock, cousin; 'tis time you were ready. By my troth, I am exceeding ill. Heigh-ho!

It is almost five o'clock, cousin; it is time you were ready. By the truth, I am exceedingly ill. Heigh-ho!

MARGARET
For a hawk, a horse, or a husband?

For a hawk, a horse, or a husband?

BEATRICE
For the letter that begins them all, H.

For the letter that begins them all, H.

MARGARET
Well, an you be not turned Turk,
there's no moresailing by the star.

Well, if you are not turned into a Turk,
there's no more sailing by that star.

BEATRICE
What means the fool, trow?

What does the fool mean?

MARGARET
Nothing I;
but God send every one their heart's desire!

I mean nothing;
but God should send everyone their heart's desire!

HERO
These gloves the Count sent me; they are an excellent perfume.

These gloves the Count sent me smell lovely.

BEATRICE
I am stuffed, cousin, I cannot smell.

I have a stuffy nose, cousin, I cannot smell.

MARGARET
A maid, and stuffed!
there's goodly catching of cold.

A maid, and stuffed!
That's a good way to catch a cold.

BEATRICE
O, God help me! God help me!
how long have you professed apprehension?

Oh God help me! God help me!
How long have you suspected this?

MARGARET

Ever since you left it.
Doth not my wit become me rarely!

Ever since you stopped.
Aren't I unusually witty today?

BEATRICE
It is not seen enough, you should wear it in your
cap. By my troth, I am sick.

It's such a rare thing, you should wear it in
your cap. By the truth, I am sick.

MARGARET
Get you some of this distilled Carduus Benedictus,
and lay it to your heart: it is the only thing for a
qualm.

Get you some of this distilled Carduus
Benedictus, and place it over your heart: it is
the only thing for sickness.

HERO
There thou prick'st her with a thistle.

There you prickle her with a thistle.

BEATRICE
Benedictus! Why benedictus?
You have some moral in this Benedictus.

Benedictus! Why benedictus?
You have some moral in this Benedictus.

MARGARET
Moral! no, by my troth, I have no moral meaning;
I meant, plain holy-thistle. You may think,
perchance, that I think you are in love: nay, by'r
lady, I am not such a fool to think what I list;
nor I list not to think what I can; nor, indeed,
I cannot think, if I would think my heart out of
thinking, that you are in love, or that you will
be in love, or that you can be in love. Yet
Benedick was such another, and now is he
become a man: he swore he would never marry;
and yet now, in despite of his heart, he eats his
meat without grudging: and how you may be
converted, I know not; but methinks you look
with your eyes as other women do.

Moral! No, by the truth, I mean no moral; I
meant, plain holy-thistle. You may think,
perhaps, that I think you are in love: no, by
your leave, I am not such a fool to think what
I suppose; nor do I suppose not to think what
I can; nor, indeed, I cannot think, if I would
think my heart out of thinking, that you are in
love, or that you will be in love, or that you
can be in love. Yet Benedick was once like that
as well, and now he has become a man: he
swore he would never marry; and yet now,
despite his heart, he eats his food without
grudging: and how you may be converted I do
not know; but I think you look with your eyes
as other women do.

BEATRICE
What pace is this that thy tongue keeps?

What are you talking about?

MARGARET
Not a false gallop.

Nothing untruthful, anyway.

[Re-enter URSULA.]

URSULA
Madam, withdraw: the prince, the count,
Signior Benedick, Don John, and all the gallants

Madam, withdraw: the prince, the count,
Sir Benedick, Don John, and all the young

of the town, are come to fetch you to church.

HERO
Help to dress me, good coz, good Meg,
good Ursula.

[Exeunt.]

noblemen of the town have come to fetch you to church.

Help to dress me, good cousin, good Meg, good Ursula.

Scene V

Another Room in LEONATO'S House

[Enter LEONATO and DOGBERRY and VERGES.]

LEONATO
What would you with me, honest neighbour?

What do you want from me, honest neighbor?

DOGBERRY
Marry, sir, I would have some confidence with you, that decerns you nearly.

Indeed sir, I would confide in you, that [he means 'concerns'] you closely.

LEONATO
Brief, I pray you;
for you see it is a busy time with me.

*Be brief, please;
for you see it is a busy time for me.*

DOGBERRY
Marry, this it is, sir.

Indeed, that it is, sir.

VERGES
Yes, in truth it is, sir.

Yes, it truly it is.

LEONATO
What is it, my good friends?

What is it, my good friends?

DOGBERRY
Goodman Verges, sir, speaks a little off the matter:an old man, sir, and his wits are not so blunt as, God help, I would desire they were; but, in faith, honest as the skin between his brows.

Goodman Verges, sir, speaks on a bit of a tangent: an old man, sir, and his wits are not so [he means 'sharp'] as, God help, I would desire they were; but, in faith, honest as the skin between his eyebrows.

VERGES
Yes, I thank God, I am as honest as any man living, that is an old man and no honester than I.

Yes, I thank God, I am as honest as any man living, that is an old man and no honester than I.

DOGBERRY
Comparisons are odorous:
palabras, neighbour Verges.

Comparisons are [he means to say 'odious', that is, distasteful, he accidentally said they were stinky]: palabras, neighbor Verges.

LEONATO
Neighbours, you are tedious.

Neighbors, you are wasting my time.

DOGBERRY

It pleases your worship to say so, but we are the poor duke's officers; but truly, for mine own part, if I were as tedious as a king, I could find in my heart to bestow it all of your worship.

LEONATO
All thy tediousness on me! ha?

DOGBERRY
Yea, an 't were a thousand pound more than 'tis; for I hear as good exclamation on your worship, as of any man in the city, and though I be but a poor man, I am glad to hear it.

VERGES
And so am I.

LEONATO
I would fain know what you have to say.

VERGES
Marry, sir, our watch to-night, excepting your worship's presence, ha' ta'en a couple of as arrant knaves as any in Messina.

DOGBERRY
A good old man, sir; he will be talking; as they say, 'when the age is in, the wit is out.' God help us! it is a world to see! Well said, i' faith, neighbour Verges: well, God's a good man; an two men ride of a horse, one must ride behind. An honest soul, i' faith, sir; by my troth he is, as ever broke bread; but God is to be worshipped: all men are not alike; alas! good neighbour.

LEONATO
Indeed, neighbour, he comes too short of you.

DOGBERRY
Gifts that God gives.

LEONATO
I must leave you.

DOGBERRY

It pleases your worship to say so, but we are the poor duke's officers; truly, though, for my own part, if I were as tedious [he has misunderstood and thought this was a compliment] as a king, I could find it in my heart to give it all to your worship.

All your time-wasting boredom on me, ha?

Yes, even if it were a thousand pounds more than it is, for I hear as good exclamation on your worship, as of any man in the city, and though I am only a poor man, I am glad to hear it.

Me too.

I would like to know what you have to say.

Indeed, sir, our watch tonight, excepting your worship's presence, has caught a pair of scoundrels at large, villainous as any in Messina.

A good old man, sir; he will be talking; as they say, 'when the age is in, the wit is out.' God help us! It is a world to see! Well said, by my faith, neighbor Verges: well, God's a good man; and when two men ride on a horse, one must ride behind. An honest soul, by my faith sir; by my truth he is, as ever broke bread; but God is to be worshipped: all men are different; alas, good neighbor!

Indeed, neighbor, he is far behind you.

Gifts that God gives.

I must leave you.

One word, sir: our watch, sir, hath indeed comprehended two aspicious persons, and we would have them this morning examined before your worship.

LEONATO
Take their examination yourself, and bring it me: I am now in great haste, as may appear unto you.

DOGBERRY
It shall be suffigance.

LEONATO
Drink some wine ere you go: fare you well.

[Enter a Messenger.]

MESSENGER
My lord, they stay for you to give your daughter to her husband.

LEONATO
I'll wait upon them: I am ready.

[Exeunt LEONATO and Messenger.]

DOGBERRY
Go, good partner, go, get you to Francis Seacoal; bid him bring his pen and inkhorn to the gaol: we are now to examination these men.

VERGES
And we must do it wisely.

DOGBERRY
We will spare for no wit, I warrant you; here's that shall drive some of them to a non-come: only get the learned writer to set down our excommunication, and meet me at the gaol.

[Exeunt.]

One word, sir: our watch, sir, has indeed [he means to say they 'apprehended' two 'suspicious' persons, what he has actually said is that they understood two lucky persons], and we would like to examine them this morning in front of your worship.

Take their examination yourself, and bring it to me: I am not in a huge hurry, as you may notice.

It shall be [he means to say 'sufficient'].

Drink some wine before you go: farewell.

My lord, they wait for you to give your daughter to her husband.

I'll go assist them: I am ready.

Go, good partner, go, get yourself to Francis Seacoal; tell him to bring his pen and inkhorn to the jail: we are now to examine these men.

And we must do it wisely.

We will spare nothing, I promise; here's what shall drive some of them to a [he means 'outcome']: only get the learned writer to set down our [he means 'communication'; 'excommunication' means kicking someone out of a religion], and meet me at the jail.

Act IV

Scene I

The Inside of a Church.

[Enter DON PEDRO, DON JOHN, LEONATO, FRIAR FRANCIS, CLAUDIO, BENEDICK, HERO, BEATRICE, &c.]

LEONATO
Come, Friar Francis, be brief: only to the plain form of marriage, and you shall recount their particular duties afterwards.

Come, Friar Francis, be brief: only give the basic version of the marriage vow, and you can discuss their particular duties afterwards.

FRIAR
You come hither, my lord, to marry this lady?

You come here, my lord, to marry this lady?

CLAUDIO
No.

No.

LEONATO
To be married to her, friar; you come to marry her.

To be married to her. You are the one who's come to marry her.

FRIAR
Lady, you come hither to be married to this count?

Lady, you come here to be married to this count?

HERO
I do.

I do.

FRIAR
If either of you know any inward impediment, why you should not be conjoined, I charge you, on your souls, to utter it.

If either of you knows any hidden obstacle, why you should not be wedded, I command you, by your souls, to say it.

CLAUDIO
Know you any, Hero?

Do you know any, Hero?

HERO
None, my lord.

No, my lord.

FRIAR
Know you any, count?

Do you know any, count?

LEONATO
I dare make his answer; none.

I dare answer for him; none.

CLAUDIO
O! what men dare do! what men may do!
What men daily do, not knowing what they do!

*Oh! What men dare do! What men may do!
What men may do! What men do daily, not
knowing what they do!*

BENEDICK
How now! Interjections? Why then, some be of
laughing, as ah! ha! he!

*What's going on? Interjections? Why then,
some are of laughter, as in ah! Hah! He!*

CLAUDIO
Stand thee by, friar. Father, by your leave:
Will you with free and unconstrained soul
Give me this maid, your daughter?

*Stand by, friar. Father, by your leave:
Will you with your free and honest soul
Give me this maiden, your daughter?*

LEONATO
As freely, son, as God did give her me.

As freely, son, as God gave her me.

CLAUDIO
And what have I to give you back whose worth

May counterpoise this rich and precious gift?

*And what do I have to give you back whose
worth
May repay this rich and precious gift?*

DON PEDRO
Nothing, unless you render her again.

Nothing, unless you give her back.

CLAUDIO
Sweet prince, you learn me noble thankfulness.

There, Leonato, take her back again:
Give not this rotten orange to your friend;
She's but the sign and semblance of her honour.
Behold! how like a maid she blushes here.
O! what authority and show of truth
Can cunning sin cover itself withal.
Comes not that blood as modest evidence
To witness simple virtue? Would you not swear,
All you that see her, that she were a maid,
By these exterior shows? But she is none:
She knows the heat of a luxurious bed;
Her blush is guiltiness, not modesty.

*Sweet prince, you teach me noble
thankfulness.
There, Leonato, take her back again:
Do not give this rotten orange to your friend;
She only looks like she is honorable.
Look! See how she blushes like a virgin here.
Oh, with what authority and show of truth
Can cunning sin hide itself!
Does that blood not come as humble evidence
To prove simple virtue? Would you not swear,
All you that see her, that she were a virgin,
By these outward signs? But she is not one:
She's been in a man's bed.
Her blushing is from guilt, not modesty.*

LEONATO
What do you mean, my lord?

What do you mean, my lord?

CLAUDIO
Not to be married,
Not to knit my soul to an approved wanton.

Not to join my soul to a loose woman.

LEONATO
Dear my lord, if you, in your own proof,
Have vanquish'd the resistance of her youth,
And made defeat of her virginity,--

My dear lord, if you, of your own will,
Have overcome the resistance of her youth,
And took her virginity, --

CLAUDIO
I know what you would say: if I have known her,

You'll say she did embrace me as a husband,
And so extenuate theforehand sin:
No, Leonato, I never tempted her with word
too large;
But, as a brother to his sister, show'd
Bashful sincerity and comely love.

I know what you would say: if I had slept with
her,
You'll say she did accept me as a husband,
And in that way excuse the sin:
No, Leonato, I never tempted her with cunning
words,
But, as a brother to his sister, showed
Bashful sincerity and appropriate love.

HERO
And seem'd I ever otherwise to you?

And did I ever seem otherwise to you?

CLAUDIO
Out on thee! Seeming! I will write against it:
You seem to me as Dian in her orb,
As chaste as is the bud ere it be blown;
But you are more intemperate in your blood
Than Venus, or those pamper'd animals
That rage in savage sensuality.

Out with you! Seeming! I will argue against it:
You seem to me as Diana in her moon,
As chaste as the flower bud before it blooms;
But you are more hot-blooded
Than Venus, or those pampered animals
That rage with savage lust.

HERO
Is my lord well, that he doth speak so wide?

Are you talking like this out of sickness?

LEONATO
Sweet prince, why speak not you?

Sweet prince, why do you not speak?

DON PEDRO
What should I speak?
I stand dishonour'd, that have gone about
To link my dear friend to a common stale.

What should I say?
I stand dishonored, that have gone around
To match my dear friend to a common slut.

LEONATO
Are these things spoken, or do I but dream?

Is this really happening, or am I dreaming?

DON JOHN
Sir, they are spoken, and these things are true.

They are spoken and they are true.

BENEDICK
This looks not like a nuptial.

This does not look like a wedding.

HERO
True! O God!

True! O God!

CLAUDIO
Leonato, stand I here? Is this the prince?
Is this the prince's brother? Is this face Hero's?
Are our eyes our own?

Leonato, do I stand here? Is this the prince?
Is this the prince's brother? Is this face
Hero's? Are our eyes our own?

LEONATO
All this is so; but what of this, my lord?

Yes this is true, but what do you mean my
lord?

CLAUDIO
Let me but move one question to your daughter,
And by that fatherly and kindly power
That you have in her, bid her answer truly.

Let me just ask one question to your daughter,
The power as a father
That you have over her, tell her to answer
truthfully.

LEONATO
I charge thee do so, as thou art my child.

I command you to do so, as you are my child.

HERO
O, God defend me! how am I beset!

What kind of catechizing call you this?

Oh, God defend me! How I am being
attacked!
What kind of cross-examination do you call
this?

CLAUDIO
To make you answer truly to your name.

To make you answer truly to your name.

HERO
Is it not Hero?
Who can blot that name
With any just reproach?

Isn't it Hero?
Who can stain that name
With any justified criticism?

CLAUDIO
Marry, that can Hero:
Hero itself can blot out Hero's virtue.
That man was he talk'd with you yesternight

Out at your window, betwixt twelve and one?
Now, if you are a maid, answer to this.

By Mary, Hero can:
Hero herself can destroy Hero's virtue.
Who was that man who talked with you last
night
Out at your window, between twelve and one?
Now, if you are a maiden, answer this.

HERO
I talk'd with no man at that hour, my lord.

I talked with no man at that hour, my lord.

DON PEDRO
Why, then are you no maiden.

Well, then you are no virgin.

Leonato, I am sorry you must hear:
upon my honour,
Myself, my brother, and this grieved count,
Did see her, hear her, at that hour last night,
Talk with a ruffian at her chamber-window;

Who hath indeed, most like a liberal villain,

Confess'd the vile encounters they have had

A thousand times in secret.

DON JOHN
Fie, fie! they are not to be nam'd, my lord,
Not to be spoke of;
There is not chastity enough in language
Without offence to utter them.
Thus, pretty lady, I am sorry for thy much
misgovernment.

CLAUDIO
O Hero! what a Hero hadst thou been,
If half thy outward graces had been plac'd
About thy thoughts and counsels of thy heart!
But fare thee well, most foul, most fair! farewell,

Thou pure impiety, and impious purity!
For thee I'll lock up all the gates of love,
And on my eyelids shall conjecture hang,
To turn all beauty into thoughts of harm,
And never shall it more be gracious.

LEONATO
Hath no man's dagger here a point for me?

[HERO swoons.]

[HERO faints.]

BEATRICE
Why, how now, cousin!
wherefore sink you down?

DON JOHN
Come, let us go.

Leonato, I am sorry you must hear:
upon my honour,
Myself, my brother, and this grieved count,
Did see her, hear her, at that hour last night,
Talk with a disreputable man at her bedroom
window;
Who has indeed, most like an enthusiastic
villain,
Confessed the disgusting encounters they have
had
A thousand times in secret.

Damn, damn! There are not to be named, my
lord, Not to be spoken of;
There is not enough chastity in language
To say them without offence.
In this way, pretty lady, I am sorry for your
terrible behavior.

Oh Hero! What a Hero you would have been,
If half your outward qualities had been placed
Around the thoughts and advice of your heart!
But fare you well, both foul and fair!
Farewell,
You pure impiety and impious purity!
For you I'll lock up all the gates of love,
And on my eyelids shall hang conjecture,
To turn all beauty into thoughts of harm,
And it will never be gracious again.

Does no one have a dagger I can stab myself
with?

Why, what's going on, cousin!
Why do you fall?

Come, let us go.

These things, come thus to light,

Smother her spirits up.

These things, coming to the surface in this way,
Have killed her.

[Exeunt DON PEDRO, DON JOHN and CLAUDIO.]

BENEDICK
How doth the lady?

How is the lady?

BEATRICE
Dead, I think! Help, uncle! Hero!
Why, Hero! Uncle! Signior Benedick! Friar!

Dead, I think! Help, uncle! Hero!
Why, Hero! Uncle! Signior Benedick! Friar!

LEONATO
O Fate! take not away thy heavy hand:
Death is the fairest cover for her shame

That may be wish'd for.

Oh Fate! Do not take away your heavy hand:
Death is the most beautiful cover for her shame
That may be wished for.

BEATRICE
How now, cousin Hero?

How are you, cousin Hero?

FRIAR
Have comfort, lady.

Have comfort, lady.

LEONATO
Dost thou look up?

Are you looking up?

FRIAR
Yea; wherefore should she not?

Yes, why should she not?

LEONATO
Wherefore!
Why, doth not every earthly thing
Cry shame upon her?
Could she here deny
The story that is printed in her blood?
Do not live, Hero; do not ope thine eyes;
For, did I think thou wouldst not quickly die,
Thought I thy spirits were stronger than thy shames,

Myself would, on the rearward of reproaches,

Strike at thy life. Griev'd I, I had but one?
Chid I for that at frugal nature's frame?

Why?!
Why, doesn't every earthly thing
Cry shame upon her?
Could she here deny
The story that is printed in her blood?
Do not live, Hero; do not open your eyes;
For, if I thought you would not quickly die,
If I thought your spirits were stronger than your shames,
I myself would, after the scolding had been finished,
Kill you myself. I grieved for having only one?
Complained about nature's stinginess?

O! one too much by thee. Why had I one?

Why ever wast thou lovely in mine eyes?
Why had I not with charitable hand
Took up a beggar's issue at my gates,
Who smirched thus, and mir'd with infamy,
I might have said, 'No part of it is mine;
This shame derives itself from unknown loins?'
But mine, and mine I lov'd, and mine I prais'd,

And mine that I was proud on, mine so much
That I myself was to myself not mine,
Valuing of her; why, she—O! she is fallen
Into a pit of ink, that the wide sea
Hath drops too few to wash her clean again,
And salt too little which may season give
To her foul-tainted flesh.

BENEDICK
Sir, sir, be patient. For my part, I am so attir'd
in wonder, I know not what to say.

BEATRICE
O! on my soul, my cousin is belied!

BENEDICK
Lady, were you her bedfellow last night?

BEATRICE
No, truly, not; although, until last night I have
this twelvemonth been her bedfellow.

LEONATO
Confirm'd, confirm'd!
O! that is stronger made,
Which was before barr'd up with ribs of iron.

Would the two Princes lie? and Claudio lie,
Who lov'd her so, that, speaking of her foulness,

Wash'd it with tears? Hence from her! let her die.

FRIAR
Hear me a little;
For I have only been silent so long,
And given way unto this course of fortune,

Oh! You were one too much! Why did I have one?
Why were you ever lovely in my eyes?
Why had I not with charitable hand
Took up a beggar's child at my gates,
Who after committing such sin,

This shame comes from an unknown father?'
But mine, and mine I loved, and mine I praised,
And mine that I was proud of, mine so much
That I myself was to myself not mine,
Valuing of her; why, she—O! she is fallen
Into a pit of ink, that the wide sea
Has too few drops to watch her clean again,
And too little salt that may give seasoning
To her disgustingly dirty flesh.

Sir, sir, be patient. For my part, I am so
mystified, I do not know what to say.

Oh! On my soul, they have lied about my
cousin!

Lady, did you share a bedroom with her last
night?

No, truly, not; although, until last night I have
been her roommate for twelve months.

Confirmed, confirmed!
Oh! That is made stronger,
Which was already barred up with bands of
iron.
Would the two Princes lies? and Claudio
Who loved her so much, that, speaking of her
sin,
Started to cry? Go away from her! Let her die.

Hear me a little;
For I have only been silent for so long,
And allowed all these things to happen,

By noting of the lady: I have mark'd
A thousand blushing apparitions
To start into her face; a thousand innocent shames

In angel whiteness bear away those blushes;
And in her eye there hath appear'd a fire,
To burn the errors that these princes hold
Against her maiden truth. Call me a fool;
Trust not my reading nor my observations,
Which with experimental seal doth warrant
The tenure of my book; trust not my age,
My reverence, calling, nor divinity,
If this sweet lady lie not guiltless here
Under some biting error.

LEONATO
Friar, it cannot be.
Thou seest that all the grace that she hath left
Is that she will not add to her damnation
A sin of perjury: she not denies it.
Why seek'st thou then to cover with excuse
That which appears in proper nakedness?

FRIAR
Lady, what man is he you are accus'd of?

HERO
They know that do accuse me, I know none;

If I know more of any man alive
Than that which maiden modesty doth warrant,
Let all my sins lack mercy! O, my father!
Prove you that any man with me convers'd

At hours unmeet, or that I yesternight
Maintain'd the change of words with any creature,
Refuse me, hate me, torture me to death.

FRIAR
There is some strange misprision in the princes.

BENEDICK
Two of them have the very bent of honour;
And if their wisdoms be misled in this,
The practice of it lives in John the bastard,

By noticing the lady: I have seen
A thousand blushing spirits
To emerge from her face; a thousand innocent shames
In angel whiteness carry away those blushes;
And in her eye there has appeared a fire,
To burn the errors that these princes hold
Against her true virginity. Call me a fool;
Do not trust my reading or my observations,
Which with experimental seal does predict
The time of my career; do not trust my age,
My reverence, calling or divinity,
If this sweet lady does not lie guiltless here
Under some terrible misunderstanding.

You see that all the grace that she has left
Is that she will not add to her damnation
A sin of perjury: she does not deny it.
Why are you looking then to cover with excuse

Lady, what man is he that they accuse you of?

They know, those who accuse me, I know nothing;
If I know more of any man alive
Than what virgin modesty is allowed to,
Let all my sins lack mercy! O, my father!
If you can prove that any man conversed with me
At unhealthy hours, or that I last night
Did anything bad with any creature,
Refuse me, hate me, torture me to death.

There is some strange misunderstanding from the princes.

Two of them are very honorable;
And if they have been misled in this business,
It must be the fault of John, the one born out of wedlock,

Whose spirits toil in frame of villanies.

Who is constantly doing evil things.

LEONATO
I know not. If they speak but truth of her,

I don't know. If they are telling the truth about her,

These hands shall tear her; if they wrong her honour,
The proudest of them shall well hear of it.
Time hath not yet so dried this blood of mine,
Nor age so eat up my invention,
Nor fortune made such havoc of my means,

My hands shall tear her; if they have done her honor wrong,
The proudest of them shall well hear of it.
Time has not yet so much dried my blood,
Nor age so eat up my invention,
Nor chance made me so poor and without resources,

Nor my bad life reft me so much of friends,
But they shall find, awak'd in such a kind,
Both strength of limb and policy of mind,
Ability in means and choice of friends,
To quit me of them throughly.

Nor my bad life took away so many friends,
But they shall find, awakened in such a way,
Both strength of body and strength of mind,
Ability in resources and choice of friends,
To cut them off forever.

FRIAR
Pause awhile,
And let my counsel sway you in this case.
Your daughter here the princes left for dead;
Let her awhile be secretly kept in,
And publish it that she is dead indeed:
Maintain a mourning ostentation;
and on your family's old monument
Hang mournful epitaphs and do all rites
That appertain unto a burial.

Hold on,
And let my advice influence you in this case.
Your daughter here the princes left for dead;
Let her be secretly kept for a while,
And spread the news that she is dead indeed:
Be obviously mournful;
and on your family's ancestral tomb
Hang mournful epitaphs and do all rites
That have to do with a burial.

LEONATO
What shall become of this? What will this do?

What shall become of this? What will this do?

FRIAR
Marry, this well carried shall on her behalf

By Mary, if you do a good job, this will on her behalf

Change slander to remorse; that is some good.

Change unjust accusation to remorse; that is some good.

But not for that dream I on this strange course,

But that is not the main reason for this strange path,

But on this travail look for greater birth.
She dying, as it must be so maintain'd,
Upon the instant that she was accus'd,
Shall be lamented, pitied and excus'd
Of every hearer; for it so falls out
That what we have we prize not to the worth
Whiles we enjoy it, but being lack'd and lost,

But look for a rebirth out of this difficulty.
She dying, as you must insist,
Upon the instant that she was accused,
Shall be cried over, pitied, and excused
By every hearer; for it happens
That we don't value fully what we have
While we enjoy it, but once it is lost and gone,

Why, then we rack the value, then we find
The virtue that possession would not show us
Whiles it was ours. So will it fare with Claudio:

When he shall hear she died upon his words,

The idea of her life shall sweetly creep
Into his study of imagination,
And every lovely organ of her life
Shall come apparell'd in more precious habit,
More moving-delicate, and full of life
Into the eye and prospect of his soul,
Than when she liv'd indeed: then shall he mourn,--

If ever love had interest in his liver,--
And wish he had not so accused her,

No, though be thought his accusation true.

Let this be so, and doubt not but success

Will fashion the event in better shape
Than I can lay it down in likelihood.
But if all aim but this be levell'd false,

The supposition of the lady's death
Will quench the wonder of her infamy:
And if it sort not well, you may conceal her,
-- As best befits her wounded reputation,--

In some reclusive and religious life,
Out of all eyes, tongues, minds, and injuries.

BENEDICK
Signior Leonato, let the friar advise you:
And though you know my inwardness and love
Is very much unto the prince and Claudio,
Yet, by mine honour, I will deal in this
As secretly and justly as your soul
Should with your body.

LEONATO
Being that I flow in grief,
The smallest twine may lead me.

FRIAR

Why, then we value it, then we find
The virtue that possession would not show us
While it was ours. It will be the same with
Claudio:
When he hears that she died because of his
words,
The idea of her life shall sweetly creep
Into his library of imagination,
And every lovely portion of her life
Shall be dressed in more precious clothing,
delicate, and full of life
Into his mind's eye,
Than when she was actually alive: then he
shall mourn, --
If love ever filled his body, --
And he will wish he had not accused her like
that,
No, even if it is thought that his accusation
was true.
Let this be what happens, and do not doubt
that success
Will mold the event in a better shape
Than I can predict.
But if everything but this turns out to be
untrue,
The supposed lady's death
Will quiet the gossip about her:
And if it does not work out, you may hide her
-- As is most suitable to her wounded
reputation, --
In some nunnery or similar religious life,
Away from all eyes, tongues, minds, and
injuries.

Sir Leonato, let the friar advise you:
And though you know my affections
Mostly lie with the prince and Claudio,
Yet, by my honor, I will deal with this
As secretly and fairly as your soul

Since I am drowning in grief,
I will grasp at the smallest rope.

'Tis well consented: presently away;
For to strange sores strangely they strain the cure.
Come, lady, die to live: this wedding day
Perhaps is but prolong'd: have patience and endure.

It is agreed: now let us go away,
For strange wounds must be strangely healed.
Your wedding day
Is perhaps only delayed: have patience and
endure.

[Exeunt FRIAR, HERO, and LEONATO.]

BENEDICK
Lady Beatrice, have you wept all this while?

Lady Beatrice, have you been crying all this
time?

BEATRICE
Yea, and I will weep a while longer.

Yes, and I will cry a little longer.

BENEDICK
I will not desire that.

I don't want that.

BEATRICE
You have no reason; I do it freely.

You have no reason; I do it freely.

BENEDICK
Surely I do believe your fair cousin is wronged.

Surely I do believe your beautiful cousin has
been wronged.

BEATRICE
Ah! how much might the man deserve of me
that would right her.

Ah! How much the man would deserve of me
that would right her.

BENEDICK
Is there any way to show such friendship?

Is there any way to show such friendship?

BEATRICE
A very even way, but no such friend.

A very good way, but I have no such friend.

BENEDICK
May a man do it?

Can a man do it?

BEATRICE
It is a man's office, but not yours.

It is a man's job, but not yours.

BENEDICK
I do love nothing in the world so well as you:
is not that strange?

I do love nothing in the world as much as I
love you: isn't that strange?

BEATRICE
As strange as the thing I know not. It were as
possible for me to say I loved nothing so well
as you; but believe me not, and yet I lie not;

As strange as the thing I do not know. It would
be as possible for me to say I loved nothing as
much as you; but do not believe me, and yet I

I confess nothing, nor I deny nothing.
I am sorry for my cousin.

do not lie; I confess nothing, and I deny nothing. I am sorry for my cousin.

BENEDICK
By my sword, Beatrice, thou lovest me.

By my sword, Beatrice, you love me.

BEATRICE
Do not swear by it, and eat it.

Do not swear by it, and eat it.

BENEDICK
I will swear by it that you love me;
and I will make him eat it that says I love not you.

I will swear by it that you love me; and I will make him eat it that says I love not you.

BEATRICE
Will you not eat your word?

Will you not eat your word?

BENEDICK
With no sauce that can be devised to it.
I protest I love thee.

With no sauce that can be devised to it. I protest that I love you.

BEATRICE
Why then, God forgive me!

Well then, God forgive me!

BENEDICK
What offence, sweet Beatrice?

What have you done sweet Beatrice?

BEATRICE
You have stayed me in a happy hour:
I was about to protest I loved you.

You have stopped me in a happy time: I was about to protest I loved you.

BENEDICK
And do it with all thy heart.

And do it with all your heart.

BEATRICE
I love you with so much of my heart that none
is left to protest.

I love you with so much of my heart that none is left to protest.

BENEDICK
Come, bid me do anything for thee.

Come, tell me to do anything for you.

BEATRICE
Kill Claudio.
BENEDICK
Ha! not for the wide world.

Kill Claudio.

Ha! Not for the whole world.

BEATRICE
You kill me to deny it. Farewell.

BENEDICK
Tarry, sweet Beatrice.

BEATRICE
I am gone, though I am here: there is no
love in you: nay, I pray you, let me go.

BENEDICK
Beatrice,--

BEATRICE
In faith, I will go.

BENEDICK
We'll be friends first.

BEATRICE
You dare easier be friends with me than fight
with mine enemy.

BENEDICK
Is Claudio thine enemy?

BEATRICE
Is he not approved in the height a villain, that
hath slandered, scorned, dishonoured my
kinswoman? O! that I were a man. What! bear
her in hand until they come to take hands, and
then, with public accusation, uncovered slander,
unmitigated rancour,--O God, that I were a man!
I would eat his heart in the market-place.

BENEDICK
Hear me, Beatrice,--

BEATRICE
Talk with a man out at a window! a proper saying!

BENEDICK
Nay, but Beatrice,--

BEATRICE
Sweet Hero! she is wronged, she is slandered,

You kill me to deny it. Farewell.

Stay, sweet Beatrice.

*I am gone, though I am here: there is no
love in you: no, please, let me go.*

Beatrice,--

I swear I will go.

We'll be friends first.

*You dare be friends more easily with me than
fight with my enemy.*

Is Claudio your enemy?

*Has he not been proved a villain, that has
slandered, scorned, and dishonored my
relative? Oh, I wish I were a man. What!
Take her hand until they come to take hands,
and then, with public accusation, speak false
words, pure harshness, -- Oh God, if I were a
man! I would eat his heart in the marketplace.*

Hear me, Beatrice,--

*Talking with a man outside the window. A
likely story!*

No, but Beatrice,--

Sweet Hero! she is wronged, she is slandered,

she is undone.

BENEDICK
Beat---

BEATRICE
Princes and counties! Surely, a princely testimony, a goodly Count Comfect; a sweet gallant, surely! O! that I were a man for his sake, or that I had any friend would be a man for my sake! But manhood is melted into cursies, valour into compliment, and men are only turned into tongue, and trim ones too: he is now as valiant as Hercules, that only tells a lie and swears it. I cannot be a man with wishing, therefore I will die a woman with grieving.

BENEDICK
Tarry, good Beatrice. By this hand, I love thee.

BEATRICE
Use it for my love some other way than swearing by it.

BENEDICK
Think you in your soul the Count Claudio hath wronged Hero?

BEATRICE
Yea, as sure is I have a thought or a soul.

BENEDICK
Enough! I am engaged, I will challenge him. I will kiss your hand, and so leave you. By this hand, Claudio shall render me a dear account. As you hear of me, so think of me. Go, comfort your cousin: I must say she is dead; and so, farewell.

[Exeunt.]

she is undone.

Beat---

Princes and countries! Surely, a princely testimony, a goodly Count Virtuous; a sweet young man, surely! Oh, if I were a man for his sake, or that I had any friend who would be a man for my sake! But manhood is melted into curses, courage into compliment, and men are only turned into tongue, and thin ones too: he is now as brave as Hercules, that only tells a lie and swears it. I cannot be a man with wishing, so I will die a woman with grieving.

Stay, good Beatrice. By this hand, I love you.

Don't swear by it, use it to prove you love me.

Are you certain that Count Claudio has wronged Hero?

Yes, as sure as I have a thought or a soul.

Enough! I will challenge him to a duel. I will kiss your hand, and leave you. By this hand, Claudio will give me satisfaction. As you hear of me, so think of me. Go, comfort your cousin: I must say she is dead; and so, farewell.

Scene II

A Prison.

[Enter DOGBERRY, VERGES, and SEXTON, in gowns; and the Watch, with CONRADE and BORACHIO.]

DOGBERRY
Is our whole dissembly appeared?

Has our whole [he means to say 'assembly'] appeared?

VERGES
O! a stool and a cushion for the sexton.

Oh! Bring a stool and a cushion for the sexton.

SEXTON
Which be the malefactors?

Who are the criminals?

DOGBERRY
Marry, that am I and my partner.

[He's misunderstood.] Indeed, that's me and my partner.

VERGES
Nay, that's certain:
we have the exhibition to examine.

*Indeed, that's certain:
we have the exhibition to examine.*

SEXTON
But which are the offenders that are to be examined?
Let them come before Master constable.

*But which are the offenders that are to be examined?
Let them come before Master constable.*

DOGBERRY
Yea, marry, let them come before me.
What is your name, friend?

*Yes, indeed, let them come in front of me.
What is your name, friend?*

BORACHIO
Borachio.

Borachio.

DOGBERRY
Pray write down Borachio. Yours, sirrah?

Please write down Borachio. Yours, sir?

CONRADE
I am a gentleman, sir, and my name is Conrade.

I am a nobleman, sir, and my name is Conrade.

DOGBERRY
Write down Master gentleman Conrade. Masters,

do you serve God?

*Write down Master gentleman Conrade. Masters,
do you serve God?*

BOTH
Yea, sir, we hope.

Yes, sir, we hope.

DOGBERRY
Write down that they hope they serve God: and write God first; for God defend but God should go before such villains! Masters, it is proved already that you are little better than false knaves, and it will go near to be thought so shortly. How answer you for yourselves?

Write down that they hope they serve God: and write God first; for God defend but God should go before such villains! Masters, it is proved already that you are little better than false knaves, and it will go near to be thought so shortly. How answer you for yourselves?

CONRADE
Marry, sir, we say we are none.

By Mary, sir, we say we are not criminals.

DOGBERRY

A marvellous witty fellow, I assure you; but I will go about with him. Come you hither, sirrah; a word in your ear: sir, I say to you, it is thought you are false knaves.

A marvelously witty fellow, I assure you; but I will go around with him. You come here, sir; a word in your ear: sir, I say to you, it is thought you are criminals.

BORACHIO
Sir, I say to you we are none.

Sir, I say we are not.

DOGBERRY
Well, stand aside. Fore God, they are both in a tale. Have you writ down, that they are none?

Well, stand aside. Before God, their stories match. Have you written down that they are not criminals?

SEXTON
Master constable, you go not the way to examine: you must call forth the watch that are their accusers.

Master constable, that's not how you examine them: you must call for the guards that are their accusers.

DOGBERRY
Yea, marry, that's the eftest way. Let the watch come forth. Masters, I charge you, in the prince's name, accuse these men.

Yes, by Mary, that's the best way. Let the watch come forth. Gentlemen, I command you, in the prince's name, accuse these men.

FIRST WATCH
This man said, sir, that Don John, the prince's brother, was a villain.

This man said, sir, that Don John, the prince's brother, was a villain.

DOGBERRY
Write down Prince John a villain. Why, this is flat perjury, to call a prince's brother villain.

Write down Prince John a villain. Why, this is flat perjury, to call a prince's brother villain.

BORACHIO

Master Constable,--

DOGBERRY
Pray thee, fellow, peace: I do not like thy look,
I promise thee.

SEXTON
What heard you him say else?

SECOND WATCH
Marry, that he had received a thousand ducats of
Don John for accusing the Lady Hero wrongfully.

DOGBERRY
Flat burglary as ever was committed.

VERGES
Yea, by the mass, that it is.

SEXTON
What else, fellow?

FIRST WATCH
And that Count Claudio did mean, upon his words,
to disgrace Hero before the whole assembly,
and not marry her.

DOGBERRY
O villain! thou wilt be condemned into everlasting
redemption for this.

SEXTON
What else?

SECOND WATCH
This is all.

SEXTON
And this is more, masters, than you can deny.
Prince John is this morning secretly stolen away:
Hero was in this manner accused, in this manner
refused, and, upon the grief of this, suddenly died.
Master Constable, let these men be bound, and
brought to Leonato's: I will go before and show
him their examination.

Master Constable,--

*Quiet, fellow: I do not like your look,
I promise you.*

What else did you hear him say?

*By Mary, that he had received a thousand
ducats from Don John for wrongfully
accusing the Lady Hero.*

That is burglary.

Yes, by God it is.

What else?

*And that Count Claudio did mean, as he said,
to disgrace Hero in front of the whole crowd,
and not marry her.*

*Oh villain! You will be condemned into
everlasting [he means 'damnation'] for this.*

What else?

That's all.

*And this is more, gentlemen, than you can
deny. Prince John has secretly run away this
morning: Hero was accused in this manner,
refused in this manner, and, full of grief from
this, suddenly died. Master Constable, let
these men be tied, and brought to Leonato's: I
will go ahead and show him their
examination.*

[Exit.]

DOGBERRY
Come, let them be opinioned.

Come, let them be [he means 'pinioned', as in gripped]

VERGES
Let them be in the hands--

Let them be in the hands--

CONRADE
Off, coxcomb!

Get off me!

DOGBERRY
God's my life! where's the sexton? let him write down the prince's officer coxcomb. Come, bind them. Thou naughty varlet!

God's my life! Where's the sexton? Let him write down the insult. Come, tie them. You naughty scoundrel!

CONRADE
Away! you are an ass; you are an ass.

Get away from me you ass; you're an ass!

DOGBERRY
Dost thou not suspect my place? Dost thou not suspect my years? O that he were here to write me down an ass! but, masters, remember that I am an ass; though it be not written down, yet forget not that I am an ass. No, thou villain, thou art full of piety, as shall be proved upon thee by good witness. I am a wise fellow; and, which is more, an officer; and, which is more, a householder; and, which is more, as pretty a piece of flesh as any in Messina; and one that knows the law, go to; and a rich fellow enough, go to; and a fellow that hath had losses; and one that hath two gowns, and everything handsome about him. Bring him away. O that I had been writ down an ass!

Do you not suspect my position? Do you not suspect my years? Oh, if he was here to write me down as an ass! But, gentlemen, remember that I am an ass; though it is not written down, yet do not forget that I am an ass. No, you villain, you are full of religious feeling, as it shall be proved of you by good witness. I am a wise fellow, and an officer, and I own property, and am quite handsome, and I know the law, and rich enough to have two sets of clothes. Bring him away. Oh, that I had been written down as an ass!

[Exeunt.]

Act V

Scene I

Before LEONATO'S House.

[Enter LEONATO and ANTONIO.]

ANTONIO
If you go on thus, you will kill yourself	*If you go on like this, you will kill yourself*
And 'tis not wisdom thus to second grief	*And it is not wise to give yourself a second grief*
Against yourself.	*Against yourself.*

LEONATO
I pray thee, cease thy counsel,	*Please, stop giving me advice,*
Which falls into mine ears as profitless	*Which I hear as pointless*
As water in a sieve: give not me counsel;	*As water in a sieve: do not give me advice;*
Nor let no comforter delight mine ear	*And do not attempt to comfort me*
But such a one whose wrongs do suit with mine:	*Unless you are someone whose wrongs are similar to mine"*
Bring me a father that so lov'd his child,	*Bring me a father that loved his child so much,*
Whose joy of her is overwhelm'd like mine,	*Whose joy in her is overwhelmed like mine,*
And bid him speak to me of patience;	*And tell him to speak to me of patience;*
Measure his woe the length and breadth of mine,	*Measure his sorrow against the dimensions of mine,*
And let it answer every strain for strain,	*And let it answer every strain for strain,*
As thus for thus and such a grief for such,	*As this way for this way and such a grief for such,*
In every lineament, branch, shape, and form:	*In every way, shape, and form:*
If such a one will smile, and stroke his beard;	*If a man like that will smile, and stroke his beard;*
Bid sorrow wag, cry 'hem' when he should groan,	*Tell sorrow to go, say 'hem' when he should wail,*
Patch grief with proverbs; make misfortune drunk	*Overcome his grief with proverbs*
With candle-wasters; bring him yet to me,	*Bring him to me,*
And I of him will gather patience.	*And I will take patience from him.*
But there is no such man; for, brother, men	*But there is no such man; for, brother, men*
Can counsel and speak comfort to that grief	*Can counsel and speak comfort to that grief*
Which they themselves not feel; but, tasting it,	*Which they themselves not feel; but, tasting it,*
Their counsel turns to passion, which before	*Their advice turns to emotion, which before*
Would give preceptial medicine to rage,	*Would give soothing medicine to rage,*
Fetter strong madness in a silken thread,	*Try to chain strong madness in a silken thread,*
Charm ache with air and agony with words.	*Magic away ache with air and agony with words.*

No, no; 'tis all men's office to speak patience

To those that wring under the load of sorrow,
But no man's virtue nor sufficiency
To be so moral when he shall endure
The like himself. Therefore give me no counsel:

My griefs cry louder than advertisement.

ANTONIO
Therein do men from children nothing differ.

LEONATO
I pray thee peace! I will be flesh and blood;
For there was never yet philosopher
That could endure the toothache patiently,
However they have writ the style of gods

And made a push at chance and sufferance.

ANTONIO
Yet bend not all the harm upon yourself;
Make those that do offend you suffer too.

LEONATO
There thou speak'st reason: nay, I will do so.

My soul doth tell me Hero is belied;
And that shall Claudio know; so shall the prince,

And all of them that thus dishonour her.

ANTONIO
Here comes the prince and Claudio hastily.

[Enter DON PEDRO and CLAUDIO.]

DON PEDRO
Good den, good den.

CLAUDIO
Good day to both of you.

LEONATO
Hear you, my lords,--

No, no; all men are supposed to speak patience
Those that struggle under the load of sorrow,
But no man's virtue can be enough
To be so moral when he shall endure
The similar problem himself. Therefore give me no advice:
I am in more grief than I show.

Men are not different from children in that respect.

Please, stop talking! I will be a human being;
For there has never yet been a philosopher
That could endure the toothache patiently,
No matter what godlike writings they have done
And talked about fortune and endurance.

Yet do not inflict all the harm on yourself;
Make sure those who have offended you suffer too

Now you're being reasonable: indeed, I will do so.
My soul tells me Hero has been lied about;
And that shall Claudio know; so shall the prince,
And all of them that dishonor her in that way.

The prince and Claudio are rushing here.

Good day, good day.

Good day to both of you.

Listen, my lords,--

DON PEDRO
We have some haste, Leonato.

We are in a hurry, Leonato.

LEONATO
Some haste, my lord! well, fare you well,
my lord:
Are you so hasty now?--well, all is one.

*Some hurry, my lord! Well, fare you well,
my lord:
Are you in such a hurry now? – Well, it is all
the same to me.*

DON PEDRO
Nay, do not quarrel with us, good old man.

No, don't quarrel with us, good old man.

ANTONIO
If he could right himself with quarrelling,
Some of us would lie low.

*If he could make things right with quarrelling,
Some of us would be dead.*

CLAUDIO
Who wrongs him?

Who wronged him?

LEONATO
Marry, thou dost wrong me; thou dissembler, thou.
Nay, never lay thy hand upon thy sword;
I fear thee not.

*By Mary, you wrong me; you liar, you.
No, never place your hand on your sword;
I am not afraid of you.*

CLAUDIO
Marry, beshrew my hand,
If it should give your age such cause of fear.
In faith, my hand meant nothing to my sword.

*By Mary, I will hold my hand still,
If it should give your oldness a reason to fear.
Honestly I never meant to go for my sword.*

LEONATO
Tush, tush, man! never fleer and jest at me:

*Enough, enough, man! Do not run away and
joke at me:*

I speak not like a dotard nor a fool,

*I am not talking like a senile old man or a
fool,*

As, under privilege of age, to brag
What I have done being young, or what would do,

*As, in the privilege of the elderly, to brag
What I did when I was young, or what I would
do,*

Were I not old. Know, Claudio, to thy head,

*If I were not old. Know, Claudio, to your
head,*

Thou hast so wrong'd mine innocent child and me

*You have so wronged my innocent child and
me*

That I am forc'd to lay my reverence by,
And, with grey hairs and bruise of many days,

*That I am forced to put aside my dignity,
And, with gray hairs and the marks of my
years,*

Do challenge thee to trial of a man.
I say thou hast belied mine innocent child:

*Do challenge you to a duel.
I say you have lied about my innocent child:*

Thy slander hath gone through and through her heart,
And she lied buried with her ancestors;
O! in a tomb where never scandal slept,
Save this of hers, fram'd by thy villany!

CLAUDIO
My villany?

LEONATO
Thine, Claudio; thine, I say.

DON PEDRO
You say not right, old man.

LEONATO
My lord, my lord, I'll prove it on his body, if he dare,
Despite his nice fence and his active practice,

His May of youth and bloom of lustihood.

CLAUDIO
Away! I will not have to do with you.

LEONATO
Canst thou so daff me?
Thou hast kill'd my child;
If thou kill'st me, boy, thou shalt kill a man.

ANTONIO
He shall kill two of us, and men indeed:
But that's no matter; let him kill one first:
Win me and wear me; let him answer me.
Come, follow me, boy; come, sir boy, come, follow me.
Sir boy, I'll whip you from your foining fence;
Nay, as I am a gentleman, I will.

LEONATO
Brother,--

ANTONIO
Content yourself. God knows I lov'd my niece;
And she is dead, slander'd to death by villains,

Your false accusation has gone through her heart,
She is buried with her ancestors;
Oh! In a tomb where scandal never slept,
Except for this one of hers, created by your villainy!

My villany?

Yours, Claudio; yours, I say.

You're wrong old man.

My lord, my lord, I'll prove it on his body, if he dare,
Despite his good swordsmanship and his regular practicing,
His youthfulness and young energy.

Go away! I will have nothing to do with you.

Can you reject me like that?
You have killed my child;
If you kill me, boy, you shall kill a man.

He shall kill two of us, and men indeed:
But that's no matter; let him kill one first:
Fight against me; let him answer me.
Come, follow me, boy; come, sir boy, come, follow me.
Sir boy, I'll whip your skills out of you;
As sure as I'm a gentleman I will.

Brother,--

Quiet. God knows I loved my niece;
And she is dead, slandered to death by villains,

That dare as well answer a man indeed

As I dare take a serpent by the tongue.
Boys, apes, braggarts, Jacks, milksops!

[A series of insults.]

LEONATO
Brother Antony,--

ANTONIO
Hold your content.
What, man! I know them, yea,
And what they weigh, even to the utmost scruple,

Scambling, out-facing, fashion-monging boys,

[Another series of insults]

That lie and cog and flout, deprave and slander,

Go antickly, show outward hideousness,

And speak off half a dozen dangerous words,
How they might hurt their enemies, if they durst;

And this is all!

LEONATO
But, brother Antony,--

ANTONIO
Come, 'tis no matter:
Do not you meddle, let me deal in this.

DON PEDRO
Gentlemen both, we will not wake your patience.

My heart is sorry for your daughter's death;
But, on my honour, she was charg'd with nothing
But what was true and very full of proof.

LEONATO
My lord, my lord--

DON PEDRO

	That have as much daring to answer to a real man
	As I dare to grab a snake by its tongue.
	Brother Antony,--
	Quiet.
	What, man! I know them, yes,
	And what they are worth, even to the furthest virtue,
	Scambling, out-facing, fashion-monging boys,
	That lie and think and reject, do depraved things and wrongfully accuse,
	Do all sorts of antics, show outward hideousness,
	And speak off half a dozen dangerous words,
	How they might hurt their enemies, if they dared;
	This is all!
	But, brother Antony,--
	Come, it is no matter:
	Do not meddle, let me deal with this.
	Both of you gentlemen, we will not test your patience.
	I'm sorry about your daughter's death.
	But on my honor, we charged her with nothing
	But what was true and well proven.
	My lord, my lord--

I will not hear you.

I don't want to hear about it.

LEONATO
No? Come, brother, away. I will be heard.--

No? Come, brother, away. I will be heard.--

ANTONIO
And shall, or some of us will smart for it.

And shall, or some of us will suffer pain for it.

[Exeunt LEONATO and ANTONIO.]

[Enter BENEDICK.]

DON PEDRO
See, see; here comes the man we went to seek.

See, see; here comes the man we went to look for.

CLAUDIO
Now, signior, what news?

Now, sir, what's happening?

BENEDICK
Good day, my lord.

Good day, my lord.

DON PEDRO
Welcome, signior: you are almost come to part almost a fray.

Welcome, sir: you have almost managed to end what was almost a conflict.

CLAUDIO
We had like to have had our two noses snapped off with two old men without teeth.

We were likely to have had both our noses snapped off by two old men without teeth.

DON PEDRO
Leonato and his brother. What think'st thou? Had we fought, I doubt we should have been too young for them.

Leonato and his brother. What do you think? If we had fought, I doubt we would have turned out to be too young for them.

BENEDICK
In a false quarrel there is no true valour. I came to seek you both.

In a false quarrel there is no true courage. I came looking for both of you.

CLAUDIO
We have been up and down to seek thee; for we are high-proof melancholy, and would fain have it beaten away. Wilt thou use thy wit?

We have been up and down looking for you; for we are in terrible melancholy, and would like to have it beaten away. Will you say something witty?

BENEDICK
It is in my scabbard; shall I draw it?
DON PEDRO

My wit is in my scabbard; shall I pull it out?

Dost thou wear thy wit by thy side?

Do you wear your wit by your side?

CLAUDIO
Never any did so, though very many have been beside their wit. I will bid thee draw, as we do the minstrels; draw, to pleasure us.

No one ever did, though very many have been beside their wit. I will tell you to pull it out, as we do tell minstrels; pull it out, to please us.

DON PEDRO
As I am an honest man, he looks pale.
Art thou sick, or angry?

As I am an honest man, he looks pale. Are you sick, or angry?

CLAUDIO
What, courage, man! What though care killed a cat, thou hast mettle enough in thee to kill care.

Have courage, man! Even if worry killed a cat, you have enough strength enough in you to kill worry.

BENEDICK
Sir, I shall meet your wit in the career, an you charge it against me. I pray you choose another subject.

Sir, I shall meet your wit in due time, if you charge it against me. Please choose another subject.

CLAUDIO
Nay then, give him another staff: this last was broke cross.

Give him another staff: this previous one has broken crossly.

DON PEDRO
By this light, he changes more and more:
I think he be angry indeed.

By this light, he changes more and more: I think he actually is angry.

CLAUDIO
If he be, he knows how to turn his girdle.

If he is, he knows how to turn it around.

BENEDICK
Shall I speak a word in your ear?

Can I speak privately with you?

CLAUDIO
God bless me from a challenge!

God save me from a challenge!

BENEDICK
[Aside to CLAUDIO.]
You are a villain, I jest not: I will make it good how you dare, with what you dare, and when you dare. Do me right, or I will protest your cowardice.

You are a villain, I am not joking: I will show how you dare, with what you dare, and when you dare. Do me right, or I will protest your cowardice.

You have killed a sweet lady, and her death shall fall heavy on you. Let me hear from you.

You have killed a sweet lady, and her death shall fall heavy on you. Let me hear from you.

CLAUDIO
Well I will meet you, so I may have good cheer.

I'll be there enjoying myself.

DON PEDRO
What, a feast, a feast?

What, a feast?

CLAUDIO
I' faith, I thank him; he hath bid me to a calf's-head and a capon, the which if I do not carve most curiously, say my knife's naught. Shall I not find a woodcock too?

In faith, I thank him; he has called me to a calf's-head and a neutered rooster, which if I do not carve most strangely, say my knife is worth nothing. Shall I not find a woodcock too?

BENEDICK
Sir, your wit ambles well; it goes easily.

Sir, your wit is walking well.

DON PEDRO
I'll tell thee how Beatrice praised thy wit the other day. I said, thou hadst a fine wit. 'True,' says she, 'a fine little one.' 'No,' said I, 'a great wit.' 'Right,' said she, 'a great gross one.' 'Nay,' said I, 'a good wit.' 'Just,' said she, 'it hurts nobody.' 'Nay,' said I, 'the gentleman is wise.' 'Certain,' said she, 'a wise gentleman.' 'Nay,' said I, 'he hath the tongues.' 'That I believe' said she, 'for he swore a thing to me on Monday night, which he forswore on Tuesday morning: there's a double tongue; there's two tongues.' Thus did she, an hour together, trans-shape thy particular virtues; yet at last she concluded with a sigh, thou wast the properest man in Italy.

I'll tell you how Beatrice praised your wit the other day. I said you ad a fine wit. 'True,' she says, 'a fine little one.' 'No,' said I, 'a large wit.' 'Right,' she said, 'a large crude wit.' 'No,' I said, 'a good wit.' 'Fair,' she said, 'it hurts nobody.' 'No,' I said, 'the gentleman is wise.' 'Certain,' she said, 'a wise gentleman.' 'No,' I said, 'he has the tongues.' 'That I believe' said she, 'for he swore a thing to me on Monday night, which he took back on Tuesday morning: there's a double tongue; there's two tongues.' In this way she, an hour together, speak of your particular virtues; yet at last she concluded with a sigh that you were the best man in Italy.

CLAUDIO
For the which she wept heartily and said she cared not.

At which point she cried hard and said she didn't care.

DON PEDRO
Yea, that she did; but yet, for all that, an if she did not hate him deadly, she would love him dearly. The old man's daughter told us all.

Yes, that she did; but yet, for all that, if she did not hate him deadly, she would love him dearly. The old man's daughter told us all.

CLAUDIO
All, all; and moreover,
God saw him when he was hid in the garden.

*All, all; and in addition,
God saw him when he was hidden in the garden.*

DON PEDRO

But when shall we set the savage bull's horns on the sensible Benedick's head?

But when shall we place the savage bull's horns on the sensible Benedick's head?

CLAUDIO
Yea, and text underneath,
'Here dwells Benedick the married man!'

Yes, and text underneath,
'Here lives Benedick the married man!'

BENEDICK
Fare you well, boy: you know my mind. I will leave you now to your gossip-like humour; you break jests as braggarts do their blades, which, God be thanked, hurt not. My lord, for your many courtesies I thank you: I must discontinue your company. Your brother the bastard is fled from Messina: you have, among you, killed a sweet and innocent lady. For my Lord Lack-beard there, he and I shall meet; and till then, peace be with him.

Farewell, boy: you know how I feel. I will leave you now to your gossiping mood; you break jokes the way braggers break their blades, which, God be thanked, do not hurt. My lord, for your many favors I thank you: I must leave your company. Your brother born out of wedlock has run from Messina: you have, among you, killed a sweet and innocent lady. For my Lord No-beard there, he and I shall meet; and till then, peace be with him.

[Exit.]

DON PEDRO
He is in earnest.
CLAUDIO
In most profound earnest; and, I'll warrant you, for the love of Beatrice.

He is serious.

In most serious earnest; and, I predict to you, for the love of Beatrice.

DON PEDRO
And hath challenged thee?

And he has challenged you?

CLAUDIO
Most sincerely.

Most sincerely.

DON PEDRO
What a pretty thing man is when he goes in his doublet and hose and leaves off his wit!

What a pretty thing man is when he puts on his clothes and leaves off his intelligence!

CLAUDIO
He is then a giant to an ape;
but then is an ape a doctor to such a man.

He is then a giant to an ape;
but then is an ape a doctor to such a man.

DON PEDRO
But, soft you; let me be: pluck up, my heart, and be sad! Did he not say my brother was fled?

But, be quiet please: leave me alone: pluck up my heart, and be sad! Did he not say my brother had run away?

[*Enter DOGBERRY, VERGES, and the Watch, with CONRADE and BORACHIO.*]

DOGBERRY
Come you, sir: if justice cannot tame you, she
shall ne'er weigh more reasons in her balance.
Nay, an you be a cursing hypocrite once, you
must be looked to.

*Come, sir: if justice cannot tame you, she
she shall never weigh any more reasons in her
scales. Indeed, if you are a cursing hypocrite
once, you must be dealt with.*

DON PEDRO
How now! two of my brother's men bound!
Borachio, one!

*What's going on? Two of my brother's men
tied! Borachio one of them!*

CLAUDIO
Hearken after their offence, my lord.

Listen to what their offence is, my lord.

DON PEDRO
Officers, what offence have these men done?

*Officers what offence have these men
committed?*

DOGBERRY
Marry, sir, they have committed false report;
moreover, they have spoken untruths; secondarily,
they are slanders; sixth and lastly, they have
belied a lady; thirdly, they have verified unjust
things; and to conclude, they are lying knaves.

*By Mary, sir, they have lied; and in addition,
they have spoken untruths; and also they have
made false accusations; sixth and lastly, they
have lied about a lady; thirdly, they have
verified unfair things; and to conclude, they
are lying criminals.*

DON PEDRO
First, I ask thee what they have done; thirdly,
I ask thee what's their offence; sixth and lastly,
why they are committed; and, to conclude,
what you lay to their charge?

*First, I ask you what they have done; thirdly,
I ask you what is their offence, sixth and
lastly, why are they in custody; and, to
conclude, what do you charge them with?*

CLAUDIO
Rightly reasoned, and in his own division; and,
by my troth, there's one meaning well suited.

*Correctly reasoned, and in his own system;
and, by my truth, there's one suitable
meaning.*

DON PEDRO
Who have you offended, masters, that you are
thus bound to your answer? this learned constable
is too cunning to be understood. What's your
offence?

*Who have you offended, gentlemen, that you
are forced to answer in this way? This
This 'learned' constable is too cunning to be
understood. What's your offence?*

BORACHIO
Sweet prince, let me go no further to mine
answer: do you hear me, and let this count kill
me. I have deceived even your very eyes:

*Sweet prince, I will answer right away: you
hear me, and let this count kill me. I have
deceived even your very eyes: what your*

what your wisdoms could not discover, these shallow fools have brought to light; who, in the night overheard me confessing to this man how Don John your brother incensed me to slander the Lady Hero; how you were brought into the orchard and saw me court Margaret in Hero's garments; how you disgraced her, when you should marry her. My villany they have upon record; which I had rather seal with my death than repeat over to my shame. The lady is dead upon mine and my master's false accusation; and, briefly, I desire nothing but the reward of a villain.

wisdoms could not discover, these shallow fools have brought to light; who, in the night overheard me confessing to this man how your brother Don John motivated me to falsely accuse the Lady Hero; how you were brought into the orchard and saw me court Margaret in Hero's clothes; how you disgraced her when you were supposed to marry her. My they have upon record; which I would rather seal with my death than repeat to my shame. The lady is dead because of my and my master's false accusation; and, briefly, I want nothing but the punishment of a villain.

DON PEDRO
Runs not this speech like iron through your blood?

Doesn't this speech run like iron through your blood?

CLAUDIO
I have drunk poison whiles he utter'd it.

I have drunk poison while he said it.

DON PEDRO
But did my brother set thee on to this?

But did my brother put you up to this?

BORACHIO
Yea; and paid me richly for the practice of it.

Yes; and paid me well for putting it into practice.

DON PEDRO
He is compos'd and fram'd of treachery:
And fled he is upon this villany.

He is made of treachery:
And has run away from this villainy.

CLAUDIO
Sweet Hero! now thy image doth appear

In the rare semblance that I lov'd it first.

Sweet Hero! Now your image appears in my mind
In the rare way that I first loved it.

DOGBERRY
Come, bring away the plaintiffs: by this time our sexton hath reformed Signior Leonato of the matter. And masters, do not forget to specify, when time and place shall serve, that I am an ass.

Come, take away the [he means to say 'defendants']: by this time our sexton has [he means to say 'informed'] Sir Leonato of the matter. And gentlemen, do not forget to specify, when the time and place is right, that I am an ass.

VERGES
Here, here comes Master Signior Leonato, and the sexton too.

Here comes Master Signior Leonato, and the sexton.

[Re-enter LEONATO, ANTONIO, and the Sexton.]

LEONATO
Which is the villain? Let me see his eyes,
That, when I note another man like him,
I may avoid him. Which of these is he?

Which is the villain? Let me see his eyes,
That, when I notice another man like him,
I may avoid him. Which of these is he?

BORACHIO
If you would know your wronger, look on me.

If you would know your wronger, look on me.

LEONATO
Art thou the slave that with thy breath hast kill'd

Mine innocent child?

Are you the slave that with your breath has killed
My innocent child?

BORACHIO
Yea, even I alone.

Yes, me alone.

LEONATO
No, not so, villain; thou beliest thyself:

Here stand a pair of honourable men;
A third is fled, that had a hand in it.
I thank you, princes, for my daughter's death:
Record it with your high and worthy deeds.
'Twas bravely done, if you bethink you of it.

No, not so, villain; you are lying about yourself:
Here stand a pair of honorable men;
A third has run away, that had a hand in it.
I thank you, princes, for my daughter's death:
Record it with your high and worthy deeds.
It was bravely done, if you think about it.

CLAUDIO
I know not how to pray your patience;
Yet I must speak. Choose your revenge yourself;

Impose me to what penance your invention
Can lay upon my sin: yet sinn'd I not
But in mistaking.

I do not know how to ask for your patience;
Yet I must speak. Choose your revenge yourself;
Impose upon me what penance your creativity
Can place upon my sin: yet I did not sin
Except by mistake.

DON PEDRO
By my soul, nor I:
And yet, to satisfy this good old man,
I would bend under any heavy weight
That he'll enjoin me to.

By my soul, nor I:
And yet, to satisfy this good old man,
I would bend under any heavy weight
That he will assign me.

LEONATO
I cannot bid you bid my daughter live;
That were impossible; but, I pray you both,

Possess the people in Messina here
How innocent she died; and if your love

I cannot tell you to tell my daughter to live;
That would be impossible; but, please, both of you,
Tell the people in Messina here
How she died innocently; and if your love

Original	Modern
Can labour aught in sad invention,	Can do such sad work,
Hang her an epitaph upon her tomb,	Hang her an epitaph upon her tomb,
And sing it to her bones: sing it to-night.	And sing it to her bones: sing it to-night.
To-morrow morning come you to my house,	Tomorrow morning come to my house,
And since you could not be my son-in-law,	And since you could not be my son-in-law,
Be yet my nephew. My brother hath a daughter,	Still become my nephew. My brother has a daughter,
Almost the copy of my child that's dead,	Almost the copy of my child that's dead,
And she alone is heir to both of us:	And she alone is heir to both of us:
Give her the right you should have given her cousin,	Give her the right you should have given her cousin,
And so dies my revenge.	And so dies my revenge.

CLAUDIO

O noble sir,	O noble sir,
Your over-kindness doth wring tears from me!	Your excessive kindness is making me tear up!
I do embrace your offer; and dispose	I do wholly accept your offer; and dispose
For henceforth of poor Claudio.	For poor Claudio from now on.

LEONATO

To-morrow then I will expect your coming;	To-morrow then I will expect your coming;
To-night I take my leave. This naughty man	To-night I take my leave. This naughty man
Shall face to face be brought to Margaret,	Shall be brought to Margaret face-to-face,
Who, I believe, was pack'd in all this wrong,	Who, I believe, was involved in this.
Hir'd to it by your brother.	Hired to it by your brother.

BORACHIO

No, by my soul she was not;	No, by my soul she was not;
Nor knew not what she did when she spoke to me;	And she did not know what she did when she spoke to me;
But always hath been just and virtuous	But has always been fair and virtuous
In anything that I do know by her.	In all my interaction with her.

DOGBERRY

Moreover, sir,--which, indeed, is not under white and black,-- this plaintiff here, the offender, did call me ass: I beseech you, let it be remembered in his punishment. And also, the watch heard them talk of one Deformed: they say he wears a key in his ear and a lock hanging by it, and borrows money in God's name, the which he hath used so long and never paid, that now men grow hard-hearted, and will lend nothing for God's sake. Pray you, examine him upon that point.	In addition, sir, -- which, indeed, is not purely black and white, -- this [he means 'defendant'] here, the offender, did call me an ass: I beg you; let it be taken into account in his punishment. And also, the watch heard them talk of one Deformed: they say he wears a key in his ear and a lock hanging by it, and borrows money in God's name, the which he has used so long and never paid, that now men grow hard-hearted, and will lend nothing for God's sake. Please, examine him upon that point.

LEONATO
I thank thee for thy care and honest pains.

I thank you for your care and honest efforts.

DOGBERRY
Your worship speaks like a most thankful and
reverent youth, and I praise God for you.

*Your worship speaks like a most thankful and
reverent youth, and I praise God for you.*

LEONATO
There's for thy pains.

Here's a reward for your efforts.

DOGBERRY
God save the foundation!

God save the foundation!

LEONATO
Go, I discharge thee of thy prisoner,
and I thank thee.

*Go, I discharge you of your prisoner,
and I thank you.*

DOGBERRY
I leave an arrant knave with your worship; which
I beseech your worship to correct yourself, for
the example of others. God keep your worship!
I wish your worship well; God restore you to
health! I humbly give you leave to depart, and
if a merry meeting may be wished, God prohibit
it! Come, neighbour.

*I leave a terrible criminal with your worship;
which I beg your worship to correct yourself,
for the example of others. God keep your
worship! I wish your worship well; God
restore you to health! I humbly give you leave
to depart, and if a merry meeting may be
wished, God prohibit it! Come, neighbor.*

[Exeunt DOGBERRY and VERGES.]

LEONATO
Until to-morrow morning, lords, farewell.

Until tomorrow, Farewell, lords.

ANTONIO
Farewell, my lords: we look for you to-morrow.

Farewel my lords, we'll see you tomorrow.

DON PEDRO
We will not fail.

We will not fail.

CLAUDIO
To-night I'll mourn with Hero.

Tonight I'll mourn with Hero.

[Exeunt DON PEDRO and CLAUDIO.]

LEONATO
[To the Watch.]
Bring you these fellows on.
We'll talk with Margaret,

*You bring these fellows with me.
We'll talk with Margaret,*

How her acquaintance grew with this lewd fellow.   *How she came to know this lewd fellow.*

[Exeunt.]

Scene II

LEONATO'S Garden.

[Enter BENEDICK and MARGARET, meeting.]

BENEDICK
Pray thee, sweet Mistress Margaret, deserve
well at my hands by helping me to the speech
of Beatrice.

*Please, sweet Miss Margaret, help me come
up with a good speech for Beatrice.*

MARGARET
Will you then write me a sonnet in praise of
my beauty?

*Will you then write me a sonnet in praise of
my beauty?*

BENEDICK
In so high a style, Margaret, that no man living
shall come over it; for, in most comely truth,
thou deservest it.

*In such a style, Margaret, that no man living
shall come over it; for, in most attractive
truth, you deserve it.*

MARGARET
To have no man come over me! why, shall I
always keep below stairs?

*To have no man come over me! Why, should
I always stay in the servant's quarters?*

BENEDICK
Thy wit is as quick as the greyhound's mouth;
it catches.

*Your wit is as quick as a greyhound dog's
mouth; it catches.*

MARGARET
And yours as blunt as the fencer's foils, which hit,
but hurt not.

*And yours as blunt as a fencer's practice
swords, which hit, but do not hurt.*

BENEDICK
A most manly wit, Margaret; it will not hurt a
woman: and so, I pray thee, call Beatrice.
I give thee the bucklers.

*A most manly wit, Margaret; it will not hurt a
woman: and so, please, call Beatrice.
I give you the bucklers.*

MARGARET
Give us the swords, we have bucklers of our own.

*Give us the swords, we have bucklers of our
own.*

BENEDICK
If you use them, Margaret, you must put in the
pikes with a vice;

*If you use them, Margaret, you must put in the
pikes with a vice;*

and they are dangerous weapons for maids.

and they are dangerous weapons for maids.

MARGARET
Well, I will call Beatrice to you,
who I think hath legs.

Well, I will call Beatrice to you,
who I think has legs.

BENEDICK
And therefore will come.

And therefore will come.

[Exit MARGARET.]

[Sings]
> The god of love,
> That sits above,
> And knows me, and knows me,
> How pitiful I deserve,--

> *The god of love,*
> *That sits above,*
> *And knows me, and knows me,*
> *How pitiful I deserve,--*

I mean, in singing: but in loving, Leander the good swimmer, Troilus the first employer of panders, and a whole book full of these quondam carpet-mongers, whose names yet run smoothly in the even road of a blank verse, why, they were never so truly turned over and over as my poor self in love. Marry, I cannot show it in rime; I have tried: I can find out no rime to 'lady' but 'baby', an innocent rhyme; for 'scorn,' 'horn', a hard rime; for 'school', 'fool',

I am terrible at poetry; the great poets were never truly turned over and over as my poor self in love. By Mary, I cannot show it in rhyme; I have tried: I can find no rhyme to 'lady' but 'baby', an innocent rhyme; for 'scorn', 'horn', a hard rhyme, for 'school', 'fool', a babbling rhyme; very ominous endings: no, I was not born under a rhyming planet, and I cannot woo in fancy ways.
for 'scorn,' 'horn', a hard rime; for 'school', 'fool',

a babbling rhyme; very ominous endings: no, I was not born under a riming planet, nor I cannot woo in festival terms.

a babbling rhyme; very ominous endings: no, I was not born under a riming planet, nor I cannot woo in festival terms.

[Enter BEATRICE.]

Sweet Beatrice,
wouldst thou come when I called thee?

Sweet Beatrice,
would you come when I called you?

BEATRICE
Yea, signior; and depart when you bid me.

Yes, sir; and leave when you bid me.

BENEDICK
O, stay but till then!

Oh, stay only till then!

BEATRICE
'Then' is spoken; fare you well now:
and yet, ere I go,

'Then' is spoken; farewell now:
farewell now: and yet, before I go, let me go

let me go with that I came for;
which is, with knowing what hath passed
between you and Claudio.

BENEDICK
Only foul words; and thereupon I will kiss thee.

let me go with what I came for;
which is, with knowing what has passed
between you and Claudio.

Only foul words; and because of them I will
kiss you.

BEATRICE
Foul words is but foul wind, and foul wind is
but foul breath, and foul breath is noisome;
therefore I will depart unkissed.

Foul words is nothing but foul wind, and foul
wind is nothing but foul breath, and foul
breath is disgusting; therefore I will depart
without being kissed.

BENEDICK
Thou hast frighted the word out of his right sense,
so forcible is thy wit. But I must tell thee plainly,
Claudio undergoes my challenge, and either I
must shortly hear from him, or I will subscribe
him a coward. And, I pray thee now, tell me, for
which of my bad parts didst thou first fall in love
with me?

You have frightened the word out of his right
sense; your wit is so forceful. But I must tell
you plainly, Claudio must face my challenge,
and I must either shortly hear from him, or
I will call him a coward. And, please now,
tell me, for which of my bad parts did you
first fall in love with me?

BEATRICE
For them all together; which maintained so politic
a state of evil that they will not admit any good
part to intermingle with them. But for which of
my good parts did you first suffer love for me?

For all of them together; which maintained
so harmoniously a state of evil that they will
not admit any good part to mix with them.
But for which of my good parts did you first
suffer love for me?

BENEDICK
'Suffer love,' a good epithet! I do suffer love
indeed, for I love thee against my will.

'Suffer love,' a good way to put it! I do suffer
love indeed, for I love you against my will.

BEATRICE
In spite of your heart, I think. Alas, poor heart!

If you spite it for my sake, I will spite it for yours;

for I will never love that which my friend hates.

In spite of your heart, I think. Alas, poor
heart!
If you spite it for my sake, I will spite it for
yours;
for I will never love that which my friend
hates.

BENEDICK
Thou and I are too wise to woo peaceably.

You and I are too wise to woo peacefully.

BEATRICE
It appears not in this confession: there's not one
wise man among twenty that will praise himself.

It does not appear so in this confession:
there's not one wise man among twenty that
will praise himself.

BENEDICK

An old, an old instance, Beatrice,
that lived in the time of good neighbours.
If a man do not erect in this age his own tomb
ere he dies, he shall live no longer in monument
than the bell rings and the widow weeps.

BEATRICE
And how long is that think you?

BENEDICK
Question: why, an hour in clamour and a quarter
in rheum: therefore is it most expedient for the
wise,--if Don Worm, his conscience, find no
impediment to the contrary,--to be the trumpet
of his own virtues, as I am to myself. So much
for praising myself, who, I myself will bear
witness, is praiseworthy. And now tell me,
how doth your cousin?

BEATRICE
Very ill.

BENEDICK
And how do you?

BEATRICE
Very ill too.

BENEDICK
Serve God, love me, and mend. There will I
leave you too, for here comes one in haste.

[Enter URSULA.]

URSULA
Madam, you must come to your uncle. Yonder's
old coil at home: it is proved, my Lady Hero hath
been falsely accused, the prince and Claudio
mightily abused; and Don John is the author of
all, who is fled and gone. Will you come presently?

BEATRICE
Will you go hear this news, signior?

BENEDICK
I will live in thy heart, die in thy lap,

---

*An old, old example, Beatrice,
that lived in the time of good neighbors.
If a man does not construct in this age his own
tomb before he dies, he shall live no longer in
a monument than the bell rings and the widow
cries.*

And how long is that, do you think?

*Question: why, an hour in chaos and a
quarter in sickness: therefore it is most useful
for the wise, -- if Don Worm, his conscience,
find no obstacle to the contrary,-- to be the
trumpet of his own virtues, as I am to myself.
So much for praising myself, who, I myself
will witness, is praiseworthy. An now tell me,
how is your cousin?*

Very unwell.

And how are you?

Very unwell too.

*Serve God, love me, and mend. There will I
leave you too, for here comes one in haste.*

*Madam, you must come to your uncle. It has
been proven that my Lady Hero has been
falsely accused, the prince and Claudio
mightily abused; and Don John is responsible
for it all, who has run away. Will you come
now?*

Will you go hear this news, sir?

I will live in your heart, die in your lap,

and be buried in thy eyes;
and moreover I will go with thee to thy uncle's.

[Exeunt.]

and be buried in your eyes;
and in addition I will go with you to your uncle's.

Scene III

The Inside of a Church

[Enter DON PEDRO, CLAUDIO, and Attendants, with music and tapers,]

CLAUDIO
Is this the monument of Leonato?

Is this the monument of Leonato?

A LORD
It is, my lord.

It is, my lord.

CLAUDIO
[Reads from a scroll.]
Done to death by slanderous tongues
Was the Hero that here lies:
Death, in guerdon of her wrongs,
Gives her fame which never dies.
So the life that died with shame
Lives in death with glorious fame.
Hang thou there upon the tomb,
Praising her when I am dumb.
Now, music, sound, and sing your solemn hymn.

Done to death by false accusation
Was the Hero that lies here:
Death, in the overcoming of her wrongs,
Gives her fame which never dies.
So the life that died with shame
Lives in death with glorious fame.
Hang you there upon the tomb,
Praising her when I am unable to speak.
Now, music, sound, and sing your solemn hymn.

SONG
Pardon, goddess of the night,
Those that slew thy virgin knight;
For the which, with songs of woe,
Round about her tomb they go.
Midnight, assist our moan;
Help us to sigh and groan,
Heavily, heavily:
Graves, yawn and yield your dead,
Till death be uttered,
Heavily, heavily.

Forgive, goddess of the night,
Those that killed your virgin knight;
For which, with songs of sadness,
Around her tomb they go.
Midnight, help us cry out in grief;
Help us to sigh and groan,
Heavily, heavily:
Graves, open and give back your dead,
Until death is said,

CLAUDIO
Now, unto thy bones good night!
Yearly will I do this rite.

Now, unto thy bones good night!
Yearly will I do this rite.

DON PEDRO
Good morrow, masters: put your torches out.

Good morning, gentlemen: put out your torches.

The wolves have prey'd; and look, the gentle day,

Before the wheels of Phoebus, round about
Dapples the drowsy east with spots of grey.
Thanks to you all, and leave us: fare you well.

CLAUDIO
Good morrow, masters: each his several way.

DON PEDRO
Come, let us hence, and put on other weeds;

And then to Leonato's we will go.

CLAUDIO
And Hymen now with luckier issue speed's,

Than this for whom we rend'red up this woe!

[Exeunt.]

The wolves have hunted; and look, the gentle day,
Ahead of the wheels of Phoebus, around about
Dapples the drowsy east with spots of grey.
Thanks to you all, and leave us: fare you well.

Good morning, masters: each of you go his different way.

Come, let us go from here, and change our clothes;
Then we will go to Leonato's.

And to the god of marriage with a luckier result,
Than this for whom we sent up this sadness!

Scene IV

A Room in LEONATO'S House.

[Enter LEONATO, ANTONIO, BENEDICK, BEATRICE, MARGARET, URSULA, FRIAR FRANCIS, and HERO.]

FRIAR
Did I not tell you she was innocent?

Didn't I tell you she was innocent?

LEONATO
So are the prince and Claudio, who accus'd her

So are the prince and Claudio, who accused her

Upon the error that you heard debated:
But Margaret was in some fault for this,
Although against her will, as it appears
In the true course of all the question.

Upon the error that you heard debated:
But Margaret was in some fault for this,
Although against her will, as it appears
In the true, complete version of the story.

ANTONIO
Well, I am glad that all things sort so well.

Well, I am glad that everything has worked out so well.

BENEDICK
And so am I, being else by faith enforc'd

And so am I, being otherwise forced by my promise

To call young Claudio to a reckoning for it.

To challenge young Claudio to a duel for it.

LEONATO
Well, daughter, and you gentlewomen all,
Withdraw into a chamber by yourselves,
And when I send for you, come hither mask'd:
The prince and Claudio promis'd by this hour

You are the other woman,
Go into a room by yourselves,
And when I send for you, come here masked:
The prince and Claudio promised that by this time

To visit me.

They would come visit me.

[Exeunt Ladies.]

You know your office, brother;
You must be father to your brother's daughter,
And give her to young Claudio.

You know your job, brother;
You must be father to your brother's daughter,
And give her to young Claudio.

ANTONIO
Which I will do with confirm'd countenance.

Which I will do with a firm face.

BENEDICK
Friar, I must entreat your pains, I think.

Friar, I must ask something from you, I think.

FRIAR
To do what, signior?

To do what, sir?

BENEDICK
To bind me, or undo me; one of them.
Signior Leonato, truth it is, good signior,
Your niece regards me with an eye of favour.

To tie me up or undo me, one of them.
Sir Leonato, it is truth, good sir,
Your niece favors me.

LEONATO
That eye my daughter lent her: 'tis most true.

That eye my daughter lent her: it is most true.

BENEDICK
And I do with an eye of love requite her.

And I do love her back.

LEONATO
The sight whereof I think, you had from me,
From Claudio, and the prince.
But what's your will?

And I think you got that from me,
From Claudio, and the prince.
But what do you want to do?

BENEDICK
Your answer, sir, is enigmatical:
But, for my will, my will is your good will
May stand with ours, this day to be conjoin'd

In the state of honourable marriage:
In which, good friar, I shall desire your help.

Your answer, sir, is enigmatical:
But, for my will, my will is your good will
May stand with ours, to be brought together
this day
In the state of honorable marriage:
That is where good friar will come in.

LEONATO
My heart is with your liking.

My heart is with your liking.

FRIAR
And my help. Here comes the prince and Claudio.

And my help. Here comes the prince and
Claudio.

[Enter DON PEDRO and CLAUDIO, with Attendants.]

DON PEDRO
Good morrow to this fair assembly.

Good morrow to this fair assembly.

LEONATO
Good morrow, prince; good morrow, Claudio:

Good morning, prince; good morning,
Claudio:

We here attend you. Are you yet determin'd

To-day to marry with my brother's daughter?

CLAUDIO
I'll hold my mind, were she an Ethiope.

LEONATO
Call her forth, brother: here's the friar ready.

[Exit ANTONIO.]

DON PEDRO
Good morrow, Benedick.
Why, what's the matter,
That you have such a February face,
So full of frost, of storm and cloudiness?

CLAUDIO
I think he thinks upon the savage bull.
Tush! fear not, man, we'll tip thy horns with gold,

And all Europa shall rejoice at thee,
As once Europa did at lusty Jove,

When he would play the noble beast in love.

BENEDICK
Bull Jove, sir, had an amiable low:
And some such strange bull leap'd your father's cow,
And got a calf in that same noble feat,
Much like to you, for you have just his bleat.

CLAUDIO
For this I owe you: here comes other reckonings.

[Re-enter ANTONIO, with the ladies masked.]

Which is the lady I must seize upon?

ANTONIO
This same is she, and I do give you her.

CLAUDIO

We are here to serve you. Are you still determined
To marry my brother's daughter today?

I wouldn't change my mind, even if she were an African.

Ask her to come, brother: the friar is here ready.

Good morning, Benedick.
Why, what's the matter,
That you have such a February face,
So full of frost, of storm and cloudiness?

I think he is thinking about the savage bull.
Enough! Do not fear, man, we'll tip your horns with gold,
And all Europe shall rejoice at you,
As once Europa [a mythological woman] did at Jove
When he carried her off in the form of a bull.

Bull Jove, sir, had a pleasant moo,
And some such strange bull leaped at your father's cow,
And got a calf in that same noble feat,
Much like to you, for you have just his bleat.

For this I owe you: here comes other reckonings.

Which is the lady I must marry?

This same is she, and I do give you her.

Why then, she's mine. Sweet, let me see your face.

Why then, she's mine. Sweet, let me see your face.

LEONATO
No, that you shall not, till you take her hand
Before this friar, and swear to marry her.

*No, that you shall not, till you take her hand
In front of this friar, and swear to marry her.*

CLAUDIO
Give me your hand: before this holy friar,
I am your husband, if you like of me.

*Give me your hand: before this holy friar,
I am your husband, if you like of me.*

HERO
And when I liv'd, I was your other wife:
[Unmasking.]
And when you lov'd, you were my other husband.

And when I lived, I was your other wife:

*And when you loved, you were my other
husband.*

CLAUDIO
Another Hero!

Another Hero!

HERO
Nothing certainer:
One Hero died defil'd, but I do live,
And surely as I live, I am a maid.

*Nothing more certain:
One Hero died defiled, but I live,
And surely as I live, I am a virgin.*

DON PEDRO
The former Hero! Hero that is dead!

The former Hero! Hero that is dead!

LEONATO
She died, my lord, but whiles her slander liv'd.

*She died, my lord, only while her false
accusation lived.*

FRIAR
All this amazement can I qualify:
When after that the holy rites are ended,
I'll tell you largely of fair Hero's death:

Meantime, let wonder seem familiar,
And to the chapel let us presently.

*I can explain all this:
When the wedding ceremony has ended,
I will tell you the whole story of beautiful
Hero's death:
Meantime, let wonder seem familiar,
And let us go to the chapel.*

BENEDICK
Soft and fair, friar. Which is Beatrice?

Soft and fair, friar. Which is Beatrice?

BEATRICE
[Unmasking.]
I answer to that name. What is your will?

That's my name. What do you want?

BENEDICK

Do not you love me?

Do you love me?

BEATRICE
Why, no; no more than reason.

No more than is reasonable.

BENEDICK
Why, then, your uncle and the prince and Claudio

Have been deceived; for they swore you did.

Why, then, your uncle and the prince and Claudio
Have been deceived; for they swore you did.

BEATRICE
Do not you love me?

Do you love me?

BENEDICK
Troth, no; no more than reason.

Truthfully, no; no more than reason.

BEATRICE
Why, then my cousin, Margaret, and Ursula,
Are much deceiv'd; for they did swear you did.

Well, then my cousin, Margaret and Ursula
Have been much deceived; for they did swear
you did.

BENEDICK
They swore that you were almost sick for me.

They swore that you were almost sick for me.

BEATRICE
They swore that you were well-nigh dead for me.

They swore that you were almost dead for me.

BENEDICK
Tis no such matter. Then you do not love me?

It is no such thing. Then you do not love me?

BEATRICE
No, truly, but in friendly recompense.

No, truly, except in a friendly manner.

LEONATO
Come, cousin, I am sure you love the gentleman.

Come, cousin, I am sure you love the
gentleman.

CLAUDIO
And I'll be sworn upon't that he loves her;
For here's a paper written in his hand,
A halting sonnet of his own pure brain,
Fashion'd to Beatrice.

And I'll swear upon it that he loves her;
For here's a paper written in his handwriting,
An awkward sonnet of his own creation,
Written to Beatrice.

HERO
And here's another,
Writ in my cousin's hand, stolen from her pocket,

Here is another,
In my cousin's handwriting, stolen from her
pocket,

Containing her affection unto Benedick.

Containing her affection for Benedick.

BENEDICK
A miracle! here's our own hands against our hearts.
Come, I will have thee;
but, by this light, I take thee for pity.

A miracle! Here's our own hands against our hearts. Come, I will have you;
but, by this light, I take you for pity.

BEATRICE
I would not deny you; but, by this good day,
I yield upon great persuasion, and partly to save
your life, for I was told you were in a consumption.

I would not deny you; but, by this good day,
I yield to great persuasion, and partly to save
your life, for I was told you were dying of
tuberculosis.

BENEDICK
Peace! I will stop your mouth.
[Kisses her.]

Enough! I will cover your mouth.
[Kisses her.]

BENEDICK
I'll tell thee what, prince; a college of witcrackers
cannout flout me out of my humour. Dost thou
think I care for a satire or an epigram? No; if
man will be beaten with brains, a' shall wear
nothing handsome about him. In brief, since I
do purpose to marry, I will think nothing to any
purpose that the world can say against it; and
therefore never flout at me for what I have said
against it, for man is a giddy thing, and this is
my conclusion. For thy part, Claudio, I did think
to have beaten thee; but, in that thou art like to
be my kinsman, live unbruised, and love my
cousin.

I'll tell you what, prince; a whole troop of
people making fun of me cannot change my
mind. Do you think I care for a satire or an
epigram? No; if man will be beaten with
brains, there shall be nothing handsome about
him. Briefly, since I do intend to marry, I will
think nothing meaningful that the world can
say against it; and therefore never make fun
of me for what I have said against it, for man
is a silly thing, and this is my conclusion.
For your part, Claudio, I did think to have
beaten you; but, since you are going to be
my relative, live unharmed, and love my
cousin.

CLAUDIO
I had well hoped thou wouldst have denied
Beatrice, that I might have cudgelled thee out
of thy single life, to make thee a double-dealer;
which, out of question, thou wilt be, if my cousin
do not look exceeding narrowly to thee.

I had hoped you would deny Beatrice, that
I might have beaten you out of your single
life, to make you a double-dealer; which, out
of the question, you will be, if my cousin does
not respond well to you.

BENEDICK
Come, come, we are friends. Let's have a dance
ere we are married, that we may lighten our own
hearts and our wives' heels.

Come, come, we are friends. Let's have a
dance before we are married, so that we may
lighten our own hearts and our wives' heels.

LEONATO
We'll have dancing afterwards.

We'll dance afterwards.

BENEDICK
First, of my word; therefore play, music!
Prince, thou art sad; get thee a wife,
get thee a wife: there is no staff more reverent
than one tipped with horn.

First, by my word; therefore play, music!
Prince, you are sad; get yourself a wife, get
yourself a wife: there is no staff more
respectable than one tipped with horn.

[Enter Messenger.]

MESSENGER
My lord, your brother John is ta'en in flight,

And brought with armed men back to Messina.
BENEDICK
Think not on him till to-morrow: I'll devise thee
brave punishments for him. Strike up, pipers!

My lord, your brother John has been
captured,
And brought with armed men back to Messina.

Do not think about him until tomorrow: I'll
come up with some good punishments for him.
Strike up, pipers!

[Dance.]

[Exeunt.]

CPSIA information can be obtained
at www.ICGtesting.com
Printed in the USA
LVHW100054170119
604241LV00001B/16/P